W9-BEC-621

HOW TO MAKE A 1,000 MISTAKES IN BUSINESS AND STILL SUCCEED

YOU MUST MAKE GOOD CRUCIAL DECISIONS — HERE'S SOME HELP

MANAGEMENT DECISIONS

The single underlying cause of success or failure in most businesses. (Chapter 2)

How you can grow your business and have a personal life, too. (Chapter 12)

MARKETING DECISIONS

The easiest and surest way to increase sales. (Chapter 4)
What to do if price is a problem. (Chapter 6)
The sales technique that almost always works. (Chapter 7)

MONEY DECISIONS

Where to find new money. (Chapter 8)
Why you need 2 sets of records—legitimately. (Chapter 9)
How to expand your hidden capacity. (Chapter 10)

GROWTH DECISIONS

Where to find the really profitable niches. (Chapter 3)
How to avoid a bad location decision. (Chapter 5)
How to find productive employees. (Chapter 11)

ATTENTION: SCHOOLS AND CORPORATIONS
Books are available at quantity discounts for bulk purchases for educational, business, or sales promotion use. For information, please write to: Group Sales, THE WRIGHT TRACK, P. O. Box 3416, Oak Park, IL 60303.

FOR A FREE COPY OF THE WRIGHT TRACK NEWSLETTER, please write to: Newsletter, THE WRIGHT TRACK, P. O. Box 3416, Oak Park, IL 60303

HOW TO MAKE A 1,000 MISTAKES IN BUSINESS AND STILL SUCCEED

The Small Business Owner's Guide to Crucial Decisions

by Harold L. Wright

THE WRIGHT TRACK

Copyright © 1990 by Harold L. Wright

All rights reserved. Printed in the United States of America. No part of this book may be used or reproduced in any manner whatsoever without written permission except in the case of brief quotations embodied in critical articles and reviews.

Published by THE WRIGHT TRACK
P. O. Box 3416, Oak Park, IL 60303

Library of Congress Catalog Card Number 89–90599
ISBN 0-9625588-0-X

Contents

Acknowledgements

1. Introducing the Crucial Decision   1

2. The Commitment Decision: Is the Grass
   Really Greener on My Side of the Street?   9

3. The "Defining the Business" Decision:
   What Business Am I In?   31

4. Marketing Focus: What Does It Look
   Like From My Customer's Viewpoint?   51

5. The Location Decision: Is There Anything
   More Important Than Location?   67

6. Pricing: Will My Customers Pay What
   I Need to Charge?   81

7. Deciding on Selling Methods:
   How Can I Sell More Without Spending More?   105

8. The Financial Decision I—Working Capital:
   Does it Take Money to Lose It?   131

Contents

9. The Financial Decision II—Profits:
   How Much Money Am I Making?   149

10. The Capacity Decision: I Must be Successful
    Because I Can't Handle Any More Business   165

11. The Personnel Decisions:
    Why Can't Employees Be More Like Us?   183

12. Decisions About the Future: What Do I Want
    to Do When I Grow Up (or Even Next Year)?   207

    Author's Notes   226

    About the Author   227

ACKNOWLEDGEMENTS

Who could have guessed that when that first small business owner asked me for help with her business that it would lead to this? This book is certainly an important landmark in the development of this new type of professional practice, one which is focused on helping small business owners become more successful.

So to client #1 and to those hundreds of clients who have followed her, I wish you continued success and I dedicate this book to you.

I don't know if I could have ever written this book without the help of Virginia McCullough. Virginia is a professional writer and a consultant to writers who has the knack of giving just the right advice to keep an author on track and to make a book better. If you're writing a book, or if you need or want to, she's someone you should meet.

John Dennis is a good friend who happens to be a creative genius in the marketing field. His ideas and his help with editing made this book a lot better.

The book was easier to do because of Lu Buckmaster and her trusty word processor.

The visual touch came from the brilliant and creative Ann Butler and her staff at Complimentary Colours who did the cover and the illustrations. Special praise goes to Frank Secord the artist who brought my favorite book worm to life to act as master of ceremonies for you.

The miracles of state of the art technology were performed by Dan Davidson and The Copyset Shop staff. They have turned desktop publishing into an art form.

My son Jim helped proofread this book and then gave me the ultimate compliment: "Dad, I enjoyed the book. I didn't think you were writing something that I'd enjoy."

Finally, Janet Taff deserves many kudos and hugs for her continuing support as well as for naming the characters in this book.

Speaking of the characters: Susan, Cindy, Alex, Bob, Dolores, Mike and Jim feel like old friends of mine by now. They represent my clients who have taught me so much about how to run a business. The characters and the events depicted are, of course, fictional. Nevertheless, I once tried to look up Mike and Jim's phone number when someone asked me if I knew a game manufacturer. I'm sure that you'll enjoy them too.

"Owning a business is one of the last great adventures which is open to everyone — and it should be fun."

"*Flipping a coin works well for a lot of decisions that are not crucial.*"

x

CHAPTER ONE

Introducing the Crucial Decision

I'm tired of seeing bright, hardworking business owners struggle simply because they've made one or two bad decisions.

George has an almost perfect business. He has found a niche providing unique budget planning services for retiring employees. His clients provide strong testimony that he truly helps people in a time of need.

George is a nice person with a blend of high energy and sound inter-personal skills. He has a well located office with good business systems and abundant working capital. He has developed outstanding marketing materials; he is an excellent sales person. The profit potential is extraordinary because he can expand the business with an inexpensive labor pool whom he trains to provide the services. He has low overhead and he can charge substantial fees. George has been in business for two years but—he has almost no clients.

George made one bad decision. He has tried to sell his

services to the wrong customers. The service is for the retiring employee, but he has been marketing his services to corporations, who employ a lot of older employees, and not to the employees themselves. It hasn't worked.

George is a clear example of an owner who has made many good decisions, and yet he finds himself with a failing business. Most small business owners make a lot of good decisions, but find themselves tripped up by one or two bad decisions.

In George's case the bad decision involved marketing but it could have involved location, working capital, employees, or any number of other areas that could make or break a business.

If you're a typical small business owner, you're highly intelligent, highly motivated, and you've worked endless hours in a field you know well and love. In my opinion, you are a cut above the rest of the working public. Why does long-term success seem just out of your reach? I'm tired of seeing bright, hardworking business owners struggle simply because they've made one or two bad decisions.

When it comes right down to it, success is based on making good decisions. That sounds obvious, but not all decisions are equally important. Some are relatively insignificant, some are important, but a few are <u>crucial</u>. Suppose you were able to isolate the crucial decisions in your business and to concentrate your efforts on being certain those are made soundly. Would your business be more successful? Of course! You can make mistake after mistake but still succeed as long as the crucial decisions are made correctly.

You can make one bad decision after another and still succeed because of good crucial decisions

Let me tell you about one of the most fouled up businesses I've ever seen. It was a carpet store and delivery service. I made my first visit "under cover" to see what it looked like from the viewpoint of a customer. Here are some of my tape recorded notes from that cloak and dagger adventure.

The carpet store is on a main street close to a major intersection in a prosperous suburb. The parking is adequate to good. A lot of activity, several crowded restaurants, and a number of impressive specialty shops give me a good feeling. There it is. Good grief, the windows are dirty!

The outside appearance could use help but at least you can tell they sell rugs, and there is a "Sale" sign. Let's go in.

The floor is dirty. The merchandise is scattered about. Most of the stuff isn't priced. The walls need painting. I want to go home!

Wait! Let's experience the attentive service, except there is no salesperson. We mill around with other customers. Finally a voice from the back, "Wait a minute. I'll be right with you." Minutes pass. Customers come and go. The salesperson appears and with a surly manner says, "Did you pick out what you wanted? If not, let me know when you do. I'll see if I can look up the prices. I'm very busy."

The more I examined the business, the worse it got. The advertising seemed designed to turn people off; the record keeping was terrible; the owner didn't seem to care about the store. But the store was making money—lots of money—mainly, I think, because two crucial decisions had been made correctly. First, the owner had picked a prime location on a street with heavy consumer traffic. And secondly, he had chosen the right business because no other carpet store could be found for miles. Because a couple of crucial decisions had been made wisely (or by dumb luck), he was thriving in spite of myriad bad management decisions.

Would the store become more profitable if it were clean and staffed by helpful, attentive people? Of course. It struck me that I had seen hundreds of businesses and had never seen one run quite so poorly. Yet it was making money. What does that tell us? Certain decisions must be *crucial* to success. Most other decisions must be less important to achieving success.

What makes the fouled up carpet store especially interesting is that it represents such an extreme. Many of the mistakes the owner was routinely making were among those I normally consider *crucial* decisions. I think of a crucial decision as one that is essential to success.

How to spot a crucial decision –
11 or 12 places to look

You must identify which decisions are crucial in your business and which are not. Many crucial decisions are obvious, and most are based on common sense. But, a few are not so obvious, and a small handful <u>defy</u> common sense. Furthermore, what constitutes a crucial decision varies from business to business.

In working with hundreds of small business owners over the past few years, I've been able to identify eleven specific areas in which crucial decisions are most often found. Each of these areas is covered in a separate chapter of this book. Some are "meat and potatoes" topics such as marketing, finances, personnel, location, and capacity. Others are not quite so easy to pin down—commitment, business focus, setting goals, and planning.

If I were asked to identify a twelfth area in which crucial decisions appear, I would name it "Recognizing Strengths and Weaknesses" or "Know Thyself." As small business owners, we wear many hats. That, after all, is part of the fun of being entrepreneurs. But, let's say one of those hats doesn't fit very well. If it's in an area where decisions are likely to be crucial, the business may get into trouble somewhere along the line.

"Blind spots" are a universal problem. If you recognize your major weaknesses you may be able to turn them into strengths. But don't ignore them. They won't just go away and if they're crucial to the success of your business, they could spell disaster. I see wonderful financiers who are the world's worst marketers. Some of the best marketers know little about managing projects. Some otherwise astute own-

ers find themselves hopelessly lost when it comes to hiring
and motivating employees.

If it's so easy, how did you ever get in such a pickle?

If most crucial decisions are based on common sense and
the business principles behind them are straightforward,
then what's the problem? The problem usually surfaces
when we try to apply these simple ideas to "real world"
business situations.

For example, any fool knows that location is the single
most important factor for the success of a small-item retail
store. But, chances are, there's a retailer (or maybe a dozen of
them) within ten minutes of you who has "hidden" himself
from his customers. Is the owner in trouble? You bet. Is he
or she just a dummy? Probably not. If you came to know that
owner, you might discover an intelligent, experienced, and
dedicated person. How could such a smart person get into
such a pickle? That's what this book is all about.

Introducing our cast of characters

Some of my clients have found themselves in situations that make their friends and relatives wonder about the value of their intelligence and experience. You'll meet these clients and learn their stories—usually as seen through their own eyes. The examples I use and the case histories I present are all based on fact, even though the names and actual businesses have been changed to protect their identity.

Our protagonists are:

Susan Andrews—she represents consultants, displaced corporate executives, and start-up businesses. You'll be with her as she decides to start her own business and struggles to find ways to keep it going.

Cindy Sorrento—a beautiful and vivacious woman who owns a moving company. Owners of service businesses, and anyone who has ever tried to straddle two careers will identify with her. You will hear about her decisions to hire and train better employees and raise more working capital.

Alex Abrams—he represents underachievers and anyone who has ever felt trapped by circumstances. Alex is a gentle soul who learned how to be a super cook in the army and proves it to the world every day.

Bob and Dolores Raferty—a couple who illustrate the challenges of retailing and the experience of a husband/wife business partnership. They are also typical of those who want a life different from the one they are presently living. You'll sit beside Bob and Dolores as they struggle to prevent a discount chain from ruining their book and card shop. If they want to retire comfortably, they have to make some crucial decisions correctly.

Mike Henninger and Jim Oberg—a team that represents manufacturers and partnerships and the perplexing problem of a successful business based on too few customers. Mike and Jim are a lot like Santa's elves. They produce toys and games and have personalities to match their business.

One thing I have learned is that small business owners are a special breed. They dare to take risks to accomplish their dreams. You'll quickly discover why I admire my clients so much. You'll probably admire them too.

Each chapter will take our heroes over a different type of decision-making hurdle. You'll find yourself rooting for your favorites, and learning from them as well. That may help you to improve some of your own decision making. It will probably enable you to further develop your business potential. That would really please me!

Want to come along? Then let's go!

CHAPTER TWO

The Commitment Decision: Is the Grass Really Greener on my Side of the Street?

The reason behind most business "failures" is a lack of owner commitment

Why are there so many business failures? The published statistics vary greatly, but it is often said that 50% of new businesses fail in the first year, and a whopping 90% fail within the first five years.

I've never been quite comfortable with these business failure figures. I don't believe there are nearly as many "failures" as the statistics suggest. Very few businesses fail. In fact, I'm continually impressed by the survival instincts of committed small business owners.

What I do see are many situations in which the owners have decided <u>not</u> to commit themselves to the business—usually a decision made early on. The question is, why?

"Success usually requires that you dive right in."

10

I believe it happens because an alternative scheme is waiting in the wings, or perhaps because the business hasn't turned out to be what the owners thought it would be.

When a person decides not to commit to something, is that a failure? I don't think so. I believe it's a decision—usually a healthy one. When you hear the stories behind the great many so called "business failures," you discover that they have less to do with the business than with the owner's personal commitment.

Making a commitment to a business involves more than a one-time decision. There are usually many points along the way where that "commitment" must be reaffirmed. And, there's no doubt that the commitment decision is a crucial one for all businesses.

What do we mean by commitment? I've seen my clients do "anything it takes" to make their businesses stay afloat during the start-up phase or other difficult periods. When I see a strong commitment decision, I know that we can make that business succeed.

Such a business will succeed because the strength of the owner's commitment will clear the obstacles away. The impact of "owner commitment" is so strong that dramatic turnarounds are common, often appearing to be "miracles."

Sometimes this strong commitment is driven by a survival instinct rather than by the desire for success. These owners don't act with commitment until they find themselves with their backs against the proverbial wall.

Let's take a closer look at commitment decisions to see how they look from a business owner's viewpoint.

The true commitment decision does not start until
the owner understands the time and money which
must be devoted to the business—
introducing Susan Andrews

I first met Susan Andrews the day after she was fired. It
was not quite as traumatic as it sounds. Susan had been an
executive in a major corporation for 15 years. Her company
had merged with another large company. Susan found
herself competing for her job with a manager from the new
owner's staff and she had lost. Susan didn't look old enough
to have had 15 years experience, and I asked her if she had
been hired as an executive at age ten. She beamed.

It's clear when talking to Susan that she is a consummate
professional. She holds an MBA, she communicates her ideas
very well and with confidence, and she isn't totally destroyed
by having lost her job. I asked Susan why she was considering
starting her own business instead of looking for a comparable
job.

"I've had the opportunity to give this a lot of thought
since the merger was announced," Susan replied. "I've
known for quite a while that it could have a direct impact on
me, so I've been doing some career planning. My specialty is
employee benefits, and I was manager of employee benefits
for the company. As a specialist, the chance of my ever being
considered for my boss's job was pretty remote. It would
probably be the same in most companies. I'd like to expand
my role—be my own boss."

Susan's idea was to become an employee benefits consultant. It wasn't a bad idea. She had been on the leading edge
of changes in the employee benefits field and she'd been

active in several employee benefits organizations. She knew this field very well and she was certainly in a position to advise other companies.

It was also evident from talking to Susan that she liked the employee benefits field. Changes had occurred during her career, and she thought the field was becoming increasingly exciting and dynamic.

One question I needed to explore with Susan was what I call the "time-money line." In other words, how much income did she have to make from her business and, equally important, how soon did she need to make it!

"I do have responsibilities," said Susan. "I'm a widow and I have two children, 8 and 10 years old. One reason I want to start my own business is to have a flexible schedule so I can spend more time with the kids.

"My salary with the company was about $60,000. I could probably live okay on about $40,000. The company was very generous. With the savings plan and severance pay, I don't really need any income for the next year. It depends on how much I need to invest in the business. I hear so much about small business failures and I worry about that a lot."

At this point I tried to give Susan some perspective about the so-called business failures. She needed to begin the process of making her commitment decision. She had identified a business about which she has knowledge and keen interest. In fact, she was excited about it. She had the financial means to get started, and she certainly had enough experience.to run a business. There were enough "ingredients" to make the decision to get going.

I suggested that Susan get started in her business so that she could learn more. Would she be able to market her services? Would she <u>like</u> operating her own business? Susan would have no way of knowing the answers to these questions, and many others, until she moved into action. It is possible that in a few months Susan would be a great success. It is also possible that she wouldn't like the business and that she would decide to do something else. That would make her a "business failure" statistic.

Fear plays an important role in building a business

"I understand," said Susan, "that I need to get started and see how it works, but frankly I'm scared. I do have a resume and a reputable headhunter has been calling me. Should I be interviewing for jobs as well?

Susan raised a number of questions that needed answers, and I have some ideas about the role of fear in building a business.

Several years ago I had the chore of introducing a panel whose members were going to present a workshop to start-up business owners. I reflected that over my career, if you counted professional practices, I had started seven businesses. Some were successful; one was a colossal flop. But as I started each one, I was scared. That initial step of making a commitment is a tough one. Furthermore, this fear has little to do with what happens afterwards, unless of course the idea of starting a business is scratched because of it.

Fear can work in many ways. I remember a client who built a good-size, successful business in just two years. The business had stopped growing and sales had not increased for the last four years. The owner obviously had a motivational problem, among other things.

After working with this owner for some time, I asked what in the world had caused the initial growth of his business. How had he built his business so successfully in the first place? What had inspired him? After all, it wasn't accidental. Something had caused him to do it. What was it? He answered in one word, "fear." He needed to get his income to the level that fit a standard of living he considered acceptable. He was afraid he might not be able to do it. Actually, "fear of survival" has built many a business. Fear is not all bad.

A business requires full commitment

Susan's other question about the wisdom of interviewing for jobs at the same time that she started her business, was much tougher, because it was related to her decision about what she wanted to do with her life.

I advised Susan to address this decision head-on because job hunting and starting a business are each more than full-time jobs. Those who try to do both, rarely succeed at either one. And if Susan perceives another corporate job as "greener grass"—something better than having her own business—then she had better examine that attitude or her business will suffer. Her new business will require her full commitment. Looking for a job could dilute that commitment.

(Susan decided to start her own business. She also had a number of job interviews and reported that she couldn't get excited about them even though they were good jobs in good companies. There was no "greener grass" for Susan. She was ready to get into action.)

Indecision will dilute owner commitment — introducing Cindy Sorrento

Cindy was not at all like I had expected her to be. I had known I was going to meet a woman who owned a household moving company. I had formed an image of a big strong woman who could hold her own with anyone. Cindy turned out to be an extremely attractive charmer who stood barely five feet tall.

Cindy and I were just starting to talk about her moving company when she said, "I've been doing some soul searching lately, and I've decided to become a professional singer."

I wasn't sure what to say. After all, she looked more like a singer than a mover, but I was confused. "Let's take this one step at a time," I said. "I'm curious. How did you get started in the moving business?"

"When I got out of school," said Cindy "I started teaching but after a couple of years I decided it wasn't for me. I went to work as the secretary to the owner of a small moving company. Over a period of seven years, I learned the moving business from the ground up. Three years ago I decided to start my own moving company."

The moving business is highly regulated and getting started wasn't easy because of all the government red tape. A new moving company is required to go through public hearings to obtain a license. Cindy faced additional resistance because she is a woman. The large moving companies made an effort to stop her at these hearings but she prevailed.

Cindy had perceived a niche in the marketplace, that of providing extra-high-quality moving services for wealthy families. This idea had worked out. Although her business had some problems, she had been making a basic living from it for the last three years. I was impressed. Now I was curious about how the singing career fit in.

It turned out that Cindy had been a teenager in the era of instant rock and roll stars and she had become one herself. She had belonged to a small singing group made up of kids from her church. They recorded a song that became a hit—it was an exciting time for her. Her group was once on the bill with the "Big Bopper" and some other stars.

It was obvious that her singing days were an important part of her life. Unfortunately, there was never a second hit and their agent "went south" with the money. But it left a spark that she wanted to rekindle and she was trying to do musical comedy and commercials. Cindy had been spending a lot of money on voice lessons, and she had arrangements with a number of agents who got her work from time to time.

"Are you really serious about your singing career?" I asked.

"I'm very serious about it," snapped Cindy, "but of course I want to build my moving business too."

I wondered if Cindy was setting herself up so that she couldn't really succeed at either venture. Many people do just that. A common trait among really successful people is that they are highly committed to whatever they do.

Commitment may be an "intangible," but it shows itself in very tangible ways. It may be measured by how one spends his or her time and what a person spends time thinking and dreaming about. There is a direct link between commitment and success. Was Cindy facing this problem? "When do you expect to get your singing career going?", I asked. "Oh, in the next couple of years," she said. "You can't really predict something like this. It's a matter of getting the breaks." Her response made me feel better about her plans. The most destructive factor in an owner's commitment can be an artificial date by which the business must perform some miracle—or else.

I heard a client announce one September that she was planning to take a teaching position the next fall if the business didn't improve. She did go back to teaching because the business didn't get better. The business stagnated because as the months passed, the client concentrated more on getting the teaching position and less on the business. At least Cindy's moving business was not saddled with a date related to her singing career. At least not yet.

(Cindy devotes most of her time to her moving business. She continues to take voice lessons, and she persists in trying to get singing jobs. But, even though she would strongly deny it, I think she treats the singing more as a hobby. However, one big break could change that.)

Commitment can be tested— introducing the squeaky chair test

When a business is in a slump, I often apply a little test to determine owner commitment. After hearing the tale of woe about the business, I will softly say, "Well, you could always go get a job." Then I listen. My client chairs both have squeaky swivels, and I am listening for the chair to squeak because the owner's back has stiffened. When I hear the chair squeak the owner is, in effect, telling me, "Hell no, I have no intention of giving up my business. They'll have to drag me away." When I hear that chair squeak I know we will succeed. The owner's head is on square, and there is no "greener grass."

I remember a client who failed the "squeaky chair test." When I asked the question about getting a job, he said that he had been considering looking for one for some time and perhaps this was the time. I offered to help him construct a resume. The only jobs he could logically hope to get were at the level of vice president of a medium-sized company or general manager at a larger company.

For 12 years he had owned a sales agency for big ticket items. His company had a profit history that looked like a roller coaster. He would earn between $30,000 and $250,000 a year and the earnings weren't predictable from one year to the next.

His family didn't know what standard of living scale they should be on, so they tended to live at about the $150,000 per year level. Whenever his earnings dropped to $30,000, they were really hurting. Although his business was quite successful by most standards, he felt like a failure. His wife had often suggested that he find a job so they could "live like normal people."

His job hunting went pretty well and he got his first interview. It was also his last, because he made his commitment decision during the interview. He decided to stay with his business. He later told me that although it looked like a good position, he realized that he would have a boss and there would be politics to deal with. He suddenly decided that there was more fun and security in his own business.

Shortly thereafter his business took off. It hasn't stopped growing since, and the roller coaster is over. There is no "greener grass" and the chair now squeaks. Over the years my client's inability to create a stable, predictable income had eroded his commitment to his business. It had made finding a job appear to be the answer. When he saw that it wasn't, he put his full effort into the business and found great success.

Moonlighting to earn money while building the business is perfectly all right and should not be confused with lack of commitment — introducing "Cats and Dogs"

Blake, a dentist and one of my clients, confided his "awful secret." He was driving a cab on the side! He said he still had two of his children in college and was not about to disrupt their education because of his business problems. The extra money he earned enabled him to keep things together.

Telling me this embarrassed him, and he was amazed when I wasn't surprised. I asked him what he would do if his dental business did not work out.

"It will work out," Blake replied. "I am a very good dentist and it's just a matter of time before I build up the business. I've been through tough times before. That doesn't scare me." Obviously his chair squeaked loud and clear. There was no "greener grass" for Blake.

I told Blake that I wasn't shocked to hear about his moonlighting because I had met many business owners who earned money in pursuits outside their regular business.

They did so until their profits started coming in. His cab driving was simply what I've come to call a "cat and dog" in memory of a client who helped me evolve the concept.

Some years ago, Janet, a photographer client of mine wanted to break into the fashion photography industry. Becoming established in fashion photography can be a long, hard road. One must create a complete and exciting portfolio and then bang on doors to establish many contacts in order to crack this industry.

My client was a very fiscally responsible person and didn't care to bankrupt herself while trying to get into this business. We came up with a plan in which, on a limited basis, actually only on Mondays, this highly trained photographer would be willing to take pictures of brides and grooms, babies, aunts, uncles, and even cats and dogs.

This plan worked and the photographer did enough business on Mondays to cover her overhead and was able to go after the fashion industry the rest of the week. Eventually she did crack the fashion industry, but alas, she discovered she didn't like it after all. (But that's another story.)

Like my photographer, Blake was simply working at something else long enough to allow his business to survive a tough time. It was part of his commitment to his business—his cat and dog.

Look carefully at the counter help in a fast food restaurant and you'll often find a young doctor or lawyer just getting started. Whenever I see such a situation, my job is a little easier because I can help set a goal based on how successful the business has to be in order for the client to quit the "cab driving."

(Blake fooled me a bit. It turned out that he really liked driving the taxi. My personal theory is that after so many years of talking to patients who couldn't talk back, he enjoyed the conversations he would strike up in the cab. It may also be that he liked the freedom of driving around after a lifetime of working in the confined area of the dental chair and the patient's mouth. Blake established goals and a time when he would stop driving a cab. However, he far exceeded his goals before he actually quit driving.)

All too often an owners commitment is to survival rather than success — introducing Alex Abrams

Alex always flunks my "squeaky chair test." He brings up closing his restaurant and finding a job quite often in our sessions. He describes the jobs in great detail. They are usually positions as a food service manager in an office or a plant where he could work from 9 to 5. However, he ignores all suggestions that he should actually look for such a job.

Alex has an overriding passion. He loves to cook, an avocation discovered while cooking in the army. After his military service, he had jobs with several restaurant chains, beginning as a cook and advancing to restaurant manager.

His restaurant has never been very profitable even though Alex works about 12 hours a day, 6 days a week. His hourly income ends up just a little higher than the rate he pays his waitresses.

Now that looks like a pretty dismal picture. You'd think that anyone would want to get out from under such a burden. If you are working over 70 hours a week, 52 weeks a year for very low pay, it should not be hard to find some "greener grass." It's no wonder the poor man talks constantly about finding another job.

A fact worth noting, however, is that Alex has owned the restaurant and has been on this schedule for the last <u>12 years</u>. While the business has never been very good, it has had some very low points where Alex has had to "scratch" to survive. In fact, Alex has become a master at survival. Whenever he is in trouble he seems to be able to scramble around and create some new revenue to hold off the creditors. I am constantly amazed at the survival instincts of the small business owner.

"The Vicious Circle" — sometimes an indication of lack of commitment

It is hard to have a discussion with Alex about improving his business. In response to almost every suggestion, Alex will relate in great detail how he already tried to do that and the numerous reasons why the idea would not work.

From a business standpoint, Alex is caught in what I call a "vicious circle." A vicious circle is a lot like chasing your tail. You can't do something because of something else and the something else traces back to the original thing you couldn't do. For example, I can't increase profits because I can't increase sales because I can't afford to advertise because I can't increase profits.

As you can see, vicious circles are very logical, but unless they are changed a business will stagnate and die. Spotting what needs to be changed and identifying the "order of change" is easier said than done, but it must be done or the business will not get better.

Can I help Alex improve his business? That has more to

do with Alex than with me. Alex is obviously committed to his business. But he seems more committed to survival than to success. (On reflection, I've often thought that Alex's decision to come to see me amounted to a new personal commitment to success on his part. Perhaps half the battle is already won.)

New goals change commitment — introducing Bob and Dolores Raferty

Bob and Dolores are intensely focused on a big decision. They own a successful book and card shop, but they are in their late fifties. They wonder how long they should continue the enterprise.

"It's funny," said Dolores, "if we worked for someone else, we would be told when we should retire. I never liked having a boss, but when it comes to this decision it would be easier."

"When would you retire?" I asked.

"I would think during the next five years," said Bob. "The finances will be important. I'm not sure if we can afford to retire. We have some savings, but most of our assets are tied up in the store and we own the building that the store is in."

I asked them what retirement looked like. Often people have no clear idea and just think retirement must be good.

"I've always wanted to write and Bob enjoys fishing and golf," Dolores replied. "We've put in some long hours in the 15 years since we started the store. I think we could occupy ourselves productively."

"Maybe we could open a smaller store in a vacation area," Bob added.

Obviously, Bob and Dolores believe there is greener grass. They believe there is something they would rather be doing than operating their business. They are undecided about what that will be, but they have decided that it should happen within the next five years.

Most people harbor some ultimate dream of how they want to spend their time. For some it may be lying on a beach and letting the surf roll over their toes. For others, it is hiking in the back country along a fresh mountain stream. My dream is playing daily matches with my hero, professional golfer Lee Trevino. We'd play for a dollar a hole and I'd actually win from time to time. Down deep, I still believe that if I could get out for more golf each summer, I could get my putting down to two strokes a hole and achieve my dream.

The way I look at it, the idea of spending all our time on the beach, in the mountains, or on the golf course is a dream. When we put a date on our dreams, they become goals. Goals change commitment.

When Bob and Dolores talk about retiring in five years, they are proposing a goal to themselves. They probably won't be able to achieve that goal unless they make the business better. If they increase their profits they will have more savings and the ability to sell their business for a higher price, thus retiring in a style they would like.

This is a case where having greener grass—a commitment outside the business—will increase commitment to the business. There is a new goal the owner needs to achieve.

Bob and Dolores were perplexed about their situation. They had, after all, been working "their tails off" for 15 years and they had a good business. It was hard for them to understand how they could make it that much better in a couple of years.

Most business owners establish a comfort level at which they want to operate their business. They will tend to continue to operate it at that level unless or until something happens that makes them change. Otherwise it's "business as usual."

I remember the professional who had had a very successful practice for 30 years. One morning he woke up and realized he was 60 years old and had made no provisions for the future. He could see himself at age 80 still trying to maintain his normal fast pace.

Within a couple of years the solo professional had taken on six associates and opened up three new offices. Interestingly enough, he hasn't slowed down a bit. He enjoys managing his new enterprise so much that he might still be doing it at age 80.

I recall another case of a twenty-year-old business that was being run by a father and son. It was very successful. The father died suddenly and the son took over. Within three years, the business had tripled in size. Both father and son were able managers so what was responsible for the growth? The business grew so dramatically because the son gave the business a different personal commitment. He envisioned a larger company and he worked tirelessly to achieve it.

"Well," said Dolores, "maybe we should have a new agenda."

(Bob and Dolores were able to grasp quickly the idea that if their good business was going to get better, they would need to change their personal commitment to it.)

A successful company with a significant problem — introducing Mike Henninger and Jim Oberg

When I was nine years old, I could recite the batting average of virtually every baseball player in the major leagues. This narrowly focused photographic memory has diminished somewhat, but I still surprise myself at times. I've never been able to account for my near obsession with baseball statistics. The best I can say is that all of us are crazy in some way and that is one way my craziness shows.

I say all this to introduce you to Jim and Mike who own a game manufacturing company. Twenty years ago Jim was an accountant and had the same disease I have—he was a baseball statistic nut. Jim put his "affliction" to better use than I did. He devised a baseball board game which uses dice and the statistics found on the back of baseball bubble gum cards.

This meant that every little kid (and big kids too) could make their bubble gum cards come alive and play actual games. For me, this invention falls just below the Salk Polio vaccine and well above the invention of television among the all-time great accomplishments.

Luckily, there were enough children that felt the same way as I, and the small company that Jim and his boyhood pal, Mike, founded was able to begin. The big break came when a large company, "Mr. Retailer," began purchasing the game and Jim and Mike's company grew rapidly. They acquired a few other games and some small game companies, but the bubble gum card game remains the most important product in the business.

Even though this is a very profitable company, there is a significant problem. More than half of the production is distributed through Mr. Retailer. This means that negotiations with Mr. Retailer control the success of the business. If Mr. Retailer ceased to be a customer the business may not survive.

Commitment makes the impossible look routine

The <u>totally committed</u> entrepreneur can make accomplishing the impossible look routine. There is an entrepreneurial instinct that supersedes almost anything else.

There was a time when the labor costs for producing Jim and Mike's games were getting out of line. The company was expanding rapidly and they hired new people. We had devised some new procedures for controlling the operation and they weren't working. The plant superintendent was called on the carpet. Nothing seemed to work.

Jim decided to go into the plant to solve the labor cost problems himself. Now Jim was a good accountant but as he readily admitted, he had no sense of how a plant should be run. Over a period of two months, he changed the production line, he changed employees, and he even changed the pop machine. When he left the plant, the labor costs were back in line.

When asked how he managed to perform this miracle, Jim replied modestly, "Talent, pure talent." In saying this Jim reinforces the principle of entrepreneurial commitment, because there is no question that Jim has no talent related to squaring away a production line. But Jim had need, perseverance, and power, and this combination will often overcome lack of talent.

Partners with a different level of commitment — A time bomb?

Jim and Mike are both committed to the business, but a year ago a large company was interested in buying them out. We spent a lot of time in discussions with the big corporation. It looked as if they would be able to sell for big bucks.

Both Jim and Mike were extremely concerned about what they would do with their lives if the sale were made. The issue was never tested because the prospective purchaser decided they could not manufacture the games as inexpensively as Jim and Mike do.

However, the opportunity to sell this business stirred up some differences in commitment that never had surfaced before. It was obvious in our discussions that Jim was doing absolutely what he wanted to do. Running the company was so much fun for him, he didn't even consider it work. The fact that he got paid for it was a bonus.

On the other hand, Mike had been an engineer and computer specialist prior to teaming up with Jim, and he did have another agenda if the business were sold. Mike expressed a desire to be a research scientist and even had a plan to acquire a Ph.D.

I consider Jim and Mike to be well adjusted partners, the key being that they are able to communicate with each other. I've seen them disagree strongly and be able to work through the problem and produce a good solution. Yet when Mike revealed his research-scientist idea, Jim found it very difficult to respond. Jim is so strongly committed to the business, he can't even understand his partner's feelings on this subject.

Owner commitment is such a basic decision in a business

that a difference in commitment between partners can be a serious problem. I've seen businesses literally pulled apart by this issue. I hope Mike and Jim's ability to communicate with each other will keep this difference from hurting the business. (I believe that when the owner is committed, the business will succeed. Jim and Mike are still clear examples of this theory in practice.)

In this chapter we've looked at a number of decisions relating to an owner's commitment to a business. We've seen that owners, particularly start-up owners, must test their commitment. They need to compare it with other alternatives to make sure they are doing what they want to be doing. We've seen how a reduced or badly focused commitment can slow a business down and how a strong commitment can enable an owner to overcome most obstacles.

Now let's look at a decision which is basic to almost every other aspect of the business. A customer asks for a new service. A supplier suggests a new product. A competitor becomes more aggressive. Your in-laws have a great idea. The direction of your business is pushed and pulled by many things, but you have to answer the question, "What business am I in?"

CHAPTER THREE

The "Defining the Business" Decision: What Business am I In?

If it's defined too broadly, your business will usually be for the birds

Suppose you are a bird doctor. You decide to sell birds as well as take care of them, and you also add a line of bird seed. Next, you invent a unique bird cage and decide to manufacture it. Your brother-in-law knows a neighborhood eccentric who can teach any bird to sing the soprano parts from the soundtrack of the movie, "An American in Paris." You decide to set up a bird training school and arrange a concert tour.

Will your business succeed? It's pretty obvious that this business is for the birds. Yet, how many of us would-be and established entrepreneurs—have at least contemplated

*"Deciding what business you're in
isn't as simple as it sounds."*

an expanded focus. Soon a vision appears. It's a combination of a professional practice, retail store, manufacturing plant, and a training school thrown in. To begin with, the chances of finding the management talent to follow such a scenario for expansion, let alone to do it well, is pretty remote.

I believe that if you define a business by stating what you do well and what you like to do, and if you stick to that definition, the business is likely to succeed. However, defining a business is not a one-time task. A business changes every day, at least a little, because it is influenced by, and interacts with, the people around it. Satisfied customers may want you to do more and give them different services. Suppliers usually want to supply more; employees will probably want to do more and get more.

If your business turns into something that you don't do well, or you don't like to do, your business will probably be for the birds too. Let's look at some of the decisions necessary to define a business and then keep it on track. I call this process "defining a business focus." One way this is done is to carefully study the competition because most good niches are found by those working within an industry. This usually happens because your customers will tell you what they need.

In this chapter you'll hear, among other things, about nominees for "bird" businesses. How about the breakfast diner that makes wedding cakes?

Doing a formal business plan can be a bad way to define a business— Susan Andrews

"Hal, I've decided how I'm going to get my business started," said Susan. "I'm going to approach it as if I were in the corporation. I'll work up a business plan and get it all laid out on paper."

My lips tightened, and my forehead wrinkled into my version of a grimace. But, how can anyone question preparing a business plan? Business plans are considered as sacred as apple pie and motherhood. They are the blueprints by which we run our lives. It is a familiar process—we've been putting them together as "reports" since grade school.

What I question is the purpose. In grade school, a plan was supposed to convince the teacher of our merits. In the corporation it was intended to convince the higher-ups of the merits of our projects in order to justify our continued employment. And if you need to convince a lender or investor to put some bucks in your business, you had better have a business plan, and it had better be a good one.

But Susan doesn't need to convince anybody of anything in order to get her business going. She has the money and the time. Is a business plan necessary? Because she is used to putting together business plans in the corporate world, maybe she should do one because that's the way she likes to work. After all it couldn't hurt, could it?

What Susan needs to do is a combination of planning and taking action. She must identify a direction for the business and then test it to see if it works. Starting a business involves making a lot of decisions all at once. Unfortunately, a person starting a venture is often at a big disadvantage when it comes to making decisions, because often they must be made based only on assumptions and guesses.

I like to have my start-up business clients get into action as soon as it is practical so they can replace assumptions with real facts when making early decisions. To the extent that developing a business plan keeps a client from testing the market place, I think a business plan can do more harm than good.

I've seen start-up business owners stare at their business plans so much that they really began to believe the assumptions and wild guesses that were contained in them. That's obviously not a healthy state of mind with which to move a business forward.

Don't get me wrong. I love business plans. But there is a big difference between "planning" and "a business plan." Planning includes the process of taking action and assessing results and a business plan doesn't. (In later chapters I'll discuss those times when a business plan is useful.)

Incidentally some of the leading outplacement companies do use business plans productively in order to discourage their clients from going into business. The purpose of outplacement companies is to help employees who have been terminated to find new employment. Many such employees have a hot idea that owning their own business might be a better answer than finding a job. Creating a business plan is a good technique to sober them up.

Ask yourself:
What business can I do well?

However she does it, Susan needs to start identifying her business and the crucial decisions she must make. The first question that requires a decision is, "What business am I in?", or in Susan's case, "What business should I be in?"

The key component in making that decision should be identifying, "What business can I do well?" The common factor found in almost every successful business is that "they do their business very well." It is virtually synonymous with "success."

The additional question should be: "What do you like to do?" When you combine "what you like to do" with "what you do well," you've defined a business that really fits you.

Susan was having a difficult time defining her business. She knew she was an employee benefits consultant, but within that description she could identify several businesses. For example, she could consult with large companies, but she knew there were many other consulting companies with whom she would be competing.

She could consult with small companies, but much that she was offering was being offered by companies that sell insurance to small business, and she doesn't want to sell insurance. She could offer a service to all employees to help them understand and get the most out of their benefits. No one was doing this, but she didn't know how she would sign up employees for the service. Susan obviously had to answer some vital questions before she could choose one preferred approach.

A classic mistake: Part time employment with no marketing plan is not a viable business definition

Susan's favorite option was to become a part time benefits manager for three different companies. She has one company in mind already, and she thinks if she sent out a letter she could find two more.

This was not the first time I had heard the part-time idea. Almost every time I work with an owner who is leaving a management job to start a consulting business this part time management idea comes up. It's a little like returning to the womb. It's a way to stay on the payroll and be in business too.

The underlying reason why defining a business as a series of part time jobs is so attractive to those starting a business is that it appears to be a way to avoid marketing. Marketing is usually an unknown risk to those starting up and therefore something to be feared. They hope that these part time jobs will turn out to be permanent so that together, it will be like having one full time job and perhaps even with a higher rate of pay.

I told Susan that taking the part-time management opportunity that she thought was available was probably a good idea. She should look at it as a good "cat and dog" which would provide income, keep her current in her field, and leave her time to market her services. But defining part-time jobs as her business could create big risks for her in the long run.

Anytime that you own a business and don't have your marketing well oiled and at the ready, you are highly at risk. I recall a vivid example of a highly successful training consultant who worked with four or five large companies at a time. For ten years he maintained high client loyalty and it seemed that whenever he lost one, a replacement would be waiting in the wings. His personal annual income was over $100,000 and he was highly respected in his field. But he had no marketing plan.

Disaster struck during a single week. Two of his clients discontinued his services and a third cut his project in half. All these actions were taken for reasons unrelated to his services, yet almost overnight his income was cut in half. Furthermore, no new clients were waiting in the wings this time. Even though the business had diminished through no fault of his own, it was a long, painful year before he was able to recover.

The business should determine the marketing— not vice versa

Susan was attempting to define her business based on the marketing problems that she perceived in each focus. The part-time jobs would require little or no marketing. Her other focuses were unattractive to her because she would have competition and/or no obvious way to get customers.

Because of her perception that she couldn't market herself and compete, Susan was trying to eliminate both these functions. The fact of the matter is that Susan, at this point, knows nothing about marketing. She has never been involved in any during her career and she doesn't want to learn. She seems willing to change her business direction in any way which would avoid marketing.

She was making decisions about the way her business would run based on assumptions and wild guesses. My perception, however, was the exact opposite of hers. I thought that Susan's services were going to be marketable despite competition, and that Susan herself would turn into an able salesperson for her services with or without my coaching. Ultimately, of course, Susan will need to determine whether this is so or not by developing and testing her marketing skills.

If she didn't want to market, I told her, perhaps she should begin looking for a full time job. Her back stiffened, the chair squeaked and the air cleared a bit. She asked me what business I thought she should be in? And I asked her, "What do you do well and what do you like to do?"

Susan said, "Oh, that's easy. I'd like to do high-level consulting with large companies. That's where my experience lies and I really enjoy it. I'd be a real expert in the field, and be able to keep in touch with my old friends. But I don't stand a chance trying to break into the field."

But it was obvious that this was an idea she wanted to test. I asked her to prepare an outline of the specific services she would be providing large companies so we could discuss it at our next meeting.

(You have just witnessed the live birth of a business. A square peg went into a square hole. She has a chance to beat the odds!)

Sometimes a business is defined too narrowly for its market — Cindy Sorrento

The 4th of July party was just breaking up when I heard water running in the downstairs bathroom. I opened the door and discovered the toilet was overflowing. After initial panic and frantic bailing, we traced the cause to a plugged up drain pipe. My emergency call to the plumber was answered by a cheerful voice who told me, "We don't do drains."

I guess I shouldn't have been surprised. After all, we've gotten used to doctors who don't make house calls and service stations that don't provide service. Why should a plumber who doesn't do drains be unusual? It's just another example of a business that doesn't do what people would expect that business to do.

While it may be cost effective for these businesses to limit the services that they provide, there is an enormous waste of marketing potential by not offering services that customers would reasonably expect. For a company like Cindy's which needs more sales, turning away logical additional business is risky indeed.

I am concerned that Cindy has defined her business too narrowly. Cindy describes her business as a high-quality, no-damage household moving business. She believes she has no competition and in a way she may be correct. If one were going to move priceless, fragile heirlooms, Cindy would be the only choice in town.

The question is, will she find enough households who

need this high-quality, more expensive service? The answer so far is yes, but just barely. She has been able to make a basic living from the business, but not much more.

Cindy is given the opportunity to bid on lots of jobs, but she loses many because her estimates are much higher than the competition. The reason for her higher prices is that she has higher costs.

Some years ago while working for another moving company she learned that damage to customer property was an accepted and "routine" part of the household moving business. Over a period of years, she worked to develop techniques that could prevent or greatly minimize damage. Her system proved very effective. In fact, Cindy had one stretch of 77 consecutive moves with "zero damage." Furthermore, since Cindy has operated her own business, she has not had a worker injured on the job.

Cindy uses more workers, equipment, and packing supplies than other movers and so her prices are higher. She believed that there were enough potential clients who would appreciate her standards and value their belongings enough to pay for the extra service.

I suggested that the business Cindy should be in was the moving business rather than the "no-damage" moving business. That specialty was too narrow for most of her potential customers to appreciate. If she defined her business as a full-service moving company she could still provide her high quality service to those who would appreciate it, but not deprive herself of the much more numerous ordinary customers and the income she needs to make her company truly viable.

This was not an idea that Cindy was ready to hear. She had a great deal of pride in her system and her accomplishments. She considered her competitors to be "wreckers" rather than movers, and she was not about to do things at their level.

An important role of an advisor is to understand the firm convictions of an owner. It is clear that at this point Cindy wants to do business her way or not at all.

(The interest and enthusiasm of the owner is so vital to a business that it can overcome most problems of the business. As Cindy continues to prove, however, a mistake in defining the business can be very costly.)

Your business changes whether you do or not

I once asked Blake, the dentist, about new developments in dentistry.

"I've been preoccupied," he replied. "And I've completely neglected continuing education courses."

I told Blake that even as a layman I was aware that the incidence of cavities was being lessened by fluoride, that there were better methods to treat gum disease, and breakthroughs in cosmetic dentistry. I also was aware of something called "TMJ", which required lengthy treatment plans to cure.

I reminded Blake of the old Bob Hope movie where Bob was playing a frontier dentist. The normal office procedure was to give a patient a slug of whiskey and then remove the tooth with a pair of pliers while Bob stood on the patient's chest for more leverage. It was a wonderful comedy scene that probably had a basis in fact.

Blake understood the point I was trying to make and responded with his usual good humor. "Actually I can't recall having used the foot on the chest procedure lately," he said, "but perhaps there are some new techniques I should be using."

A business must be able to recognize and react to change. If the city starts to tear up the street in front of your store, you're forced to notice and react. But sometimes the change is more subtle and harder to detect. For example, a large corporation started to give away what one of my clients was trying to sell. Sound devastating? Our solution, once we recognized what was happening, was to shift our marketing focus to sell our services to those corporations

If a business should be based on what it does well, should Alex go back to being a cook?

When I first started working with Alex he didn't have time to come to my office so we would meet in the kitchen of his restaurant. He would usually fix me something to eat, a fringe benefit to being his consultant. The reason I consented to this arrangement was that Alex was a great cook. The meals he served were delicious.

Of course, Alex did very little of the cooking at his restaurant himself because he had hired short-order cooks. Alex was busy with management duties which he defined as buying food, planning the menus, and handling the cash register. Much of his time was spent talking to bill collectors and thinking up new promotional schemes.

The restaurant was open for breakfast, lunch, and

dinner Monday through Saturday. When I asked what meal was the busiest, there was no hesitation. It was breakfast. On Monday through Friday the receipts at breakfast were often more than lunch and dinner combined.

Alex had tried all sorts of things to boost afternoon and evening business. He had business men's specials, two for ones, and special seasonal meals. He even got a license to serve wine. Nothing helped. Alex had some catering business and was making some extra money by baking wedding cakes. So basically, the restaurant was a breakfast place that baked wedding cakes! That isn't the business Alex had wanted to be in, but those were the only parts that were working.

Alex started the restaurant 12 years earlier to capitalize on his culinary skills. Yet Alex was not cooking. Perhaps that was part of the problem.

Perhaps the food was not good enough because the short-order cooks weren't highly skilled. Could it be that simple? The cooks were good at breakfast because the preparation of the more limited breakfast menu was within their ability.

Alex gets very defensive at any suggestion that his food is not the best. Most of his menu is based on his own recipes. He admits there are several dishes he purchases precooked and frozen—mostly fish because his cooks have problems preparing certain "delicate" items.

What comes through loud and clear is that Alex wants to have a sit down restaurant that serves great food for reasonable prices. He blames his lack of success on many factors, some of which may be valid. But it never before crossed his mind that his food might not be top quality. He is genuinely shocked. He is doing catering and wedding cakes and many other things just to survive. Alex knows what he wants the business to be and he <u>will</u> make the food the quality he thinks it should be.

(Many businesses are based on the specific talents and strengths of the owner. As the business develops, the owner's attention is required in areas unrelated to those special talents. Sometimes it's necessary to refocus to get back to the basic strengths of the business.)

The really profitable new business directions are most often discovered from within an industry, not from the outside looking in. They are often suggested by customers.

Bob and Dolores' business has little resemblance to the book store they opened ten years ago. Originally the business was based on Dolores' love for and knowledge of books. During their first year, however, they added a small line of greeting cards, which grew to many racks of cards. In spite of lots of competition, including a franchise card shop, the card business is going well, and this has created a continuous flow of customers, especially during holiday seasons.

A couple of years later, at the request of a few nearby businesses, Bob and Dolores started to carry some office supplies. The office supply business has also grown and has provided a good sales balance during non-holiday months.

This is not an unusual story. Often, an established business enters a new field because customers have requested it. Sometimes the new pursuit may not be particularly profitable, but it is continued as a customer service because a good customer has asked for it. These "customer services" can be clues to new, highly profitable niches.

Some years ago one of my clients was asked to provide a special telephone answering service for the car phones of one of his major customers. He was able to provide the service, but he had a difficult time pricing it because no one seemed to do it in his locale. He ended up calling around the country before he could come up with the going price.

When he analyzed his costs he found, to his great surprise, that they were only 10% of the going price. This was too interesting to ignore, and he and I looked hard at this new service. Ultimately, my client found he needed to invest $30,000 to do the service properly. That was a significant investment for him at that time, but he decided to go ahead and do it.

It turned out to be an excellent decision. Within 6 months the $30,000 was recouped and three years later, this "customer service" was accounting for as much profit as all the rest of his business combined.

This example could be called a "routine" story of great success, because this is a common way for success to be achieved. Instead of chasing "pie in the sky," it focuses on something right under your nose. Often it's hard to see something that close, but listening to your customers is a good way to start looking. What do they need? What do they need done better? More cost effectively?

The key to growth for Bob and Dolores is likely to be found in the businesses they are already in. They are in three businesses: books, cards, and office supplies. I asked Bob and Dolores what opportunities they saw in each.

"Discounters have really hurt us in both books and office supplies," said Bob. "I often wonder if we should be in either business. On the other hand, I can see new directions we could go in with both lines."

I asked Bob what directions he had in mind. "In the book business we could put more emphasis in certain popular categories such as travel, cooking, and children's books," said Bob. "And we could expand our computer supplies and even sell computer software. We get calls for specialty books and for computer-related items all the time."

Then I asked if there was any growth potential in the card business. This was Dolores' special interest and she was quick to respond that party goods seemed to her to be the next logical expansion. It was clear that selling greeting cards was the most successful part of the business. Half the town shopped for cards in their store.

Dolores said it very clearly: "We are a gift shop. We are primarily in the business of selling people gifts." She is right and that is a major clue for future growth.

(Bob and Dolores have more solid choices for business focus than most businesses have. By understanding what is working and why, they can grow from strength with less risk and more potential.)

Defining a Business is a Continuous Process— Mike Henninger and Jim Oberg

Success! By almost any measure Mike and Jim have a very successful business. They are happy running their game company, and it is making them more money than they ever expected it would.

Panic! Mike and Jim could be out of business and maybe even bankrupt within a short period of time, if one or two people made decisions that excluded them. Yes, I'm describing the same business at the same point in time—with fabulous success and ultimate disaster existing side by side. Let me explain.

Mike and Jim are in the business of making games for kids. Notice I didn't say "making and selling," because Mike and Jim have developed virtually no marketing function in their business.

Everything that Mike and Jim produce is sold to distributors. In fact most is sold to one distributor, a chain of stores known as "Mr. Retailer." Mr. Retailer's business has grown over the last few years, and Mike and Jim have grown along with it. But each year there is a negotiation with "Mr. Retailer" and each year there is very real possibility that it could all end. For their own peace of mind, Jim and Mike have to redefine their business—and soon!

It is not a new issue for Mike and Jim. Over the years they have bought out a few smaller manufacturers in an attempt to diversify, but nothing has worked. We needed to find something that would.

In situations like this, I have discovered that many approaches are workable. Usually, the most important factor is the interest the owner takes in the new business focus.

I asked Mike and Jim to make a list of all the approaches they had ever considered. We would review them and perhaps come up with an answer. It turned out to be a rather long list. Some possibilities were easy to eliminate. They had gone the route of buying up smaller companies and they had bought someone else's problems on each occasion.

Another approach Mike and Jim had tried was to set

up their own sales force and sell directly to retailers. This failed for several reasons, but primarily because they did not have enough different games to make up a product line. The salesmen didn't have enough different items to sell. They could have expanded their line, but that would mean going into direct competition with several companies that were a hundred times larger than theirs.

The partners had also considered making products other than games. They had actually produced prototypes and test runs on at least six different products all of which were outside their usual business focus. The most successful was in the plumbing field but all of them had fizzled, and they had cost a lot of money to develop.

Mike and Jim were able to convince me that none of the above would work, and if I was inclined to get discouraged easily, I could have advised them to sell out while they could. Take the money and run.

Then Jim said, "Here's another real loser. We developed this baseball game that is somewhat related to our bubble gum baseball card game. It's more complicated and a lot more expensive because we have to supply all the statistics."

"Yes, it's a great game." Mike added. "We play it ourselves. You have to make all the decisions that a big league manager would make. We showed it to Mr. Retailer but he turned it down. Too high priced. Too complicated for kids. Not enough of a market."

That idea rang a bell with me. This was a game that was based on the design of their original successful game. They actually played it themselves. It appeared that many baseball fans would be potential customers, even though it may not fit Mr. Retailer's market. The fact that it was a higher priced game intrigued me. Also new statistics would be available to sell each year. Perhaps it was a mistake to try to sell it through retail stores. Perhaps the game should be sold directly to the game players.

I found myself saying two little words that changed a business forever, "<u>Mail</u> <u>Order</u>."

(There are many ways in which a small business has a big edge over larger companies. For one, a small manufacturer doesn't have to have a huge market to be successful. It only has to have a way to get to its market. Mr. Retailer wasn't interested in products that were too specialized, but that doesn't mean a market isn't there. Mike and Jim may have found the path to diversify.)

Once you have your business defined, you've made a quantum leap toward business success. You can easily leap past success if you ignore what your business looks like to your customer. Changing your focus to look at your business through your customer's eyes is much harder for most of us than it should be. In the next chapter, we'll explore some important examples of the customer's viewpoint.

CHAPTER FOUR

Marketing Focus: What Does It Look Like From My Customer's Point Of View?

Introducing: the black box theory

A friend of mine told me that at one time his wife spent money they didn't have. When he asked her not to do that, she spent even more. But, since the arrival of the "black box," he and his wife plan their monthly budget together and they stick to it. What a wonderful solution to a common problem! Chances are, a "black box" would make your relationships happier too.

Fred, a financial planner, had worked out some neat ideas to encourage people to save money. Since the techniques that he suggested sounded like a lot of hard work, people were not lined up in front of his office to try them out. Yet the benefits of learning how to save money could be

"Discovering your customer's point of view may require some careful examination."

52

wonderful.

As long as Fred told his potential clients about the techniques he used, he had very few clients. Once he put those techniques in a "black box" and simply told his clients the results they could expect, business boomed.

Potential customers are attracted to what they get and not how they get it. The "black box" could contain Fred's ideas, or a pill, a psychiatrist's advice, a book, a computer or many other things you could name. It wouldn't matter as long as it produced the benefits.

When we define our business we naturally look at the features that we offer, but using these features to try to sell our goods and services is often a mistake. We need to look at what we offer from our customer's point of view and often the best way to do this is to substitute "black box" each time you talk about a feature of your business. This leaves you free to concentrate on the benefits available to your customers.

Determining what your business looks like from the customer's viewpoint is much more difficult than it sounds. Most small business owners are intensely invested in what they do and how they do it. For example, a baker may tell you about the high quality ingredients used in baking his pies. But all that needs to be said is, "Would you like to try my pie?"

Let's see how our friends handle this important marketing decision.

Think benefits not features! —
Susan Andrews

Susan was bubbling with excitement. "I did what you asked and prepared a list of services that I can provide to large companies." said Susan. "Then I put it in a brochure format. I thought I would send it to the 'Fortune 500.' That should get me all kinds of business."

I looked over the draft of the brochure that Susan had prepared. I was impressed. Susan had accumulated much valuable experience on her corporate job. She had been involved in developing computer systems, implementing changes in employee benefit law, devising systems to cut costs, communicating with employees, etc. However, I told Susan that I thought the brochure might be useful to send to people that she already knew, but I didn't think it would be effective to send it cold to the "Fortune 500."

Susan was upset. "What's wrong with the brochure?", she asked as she pulled out brochures from a number of large consulting companies. "Isn't mine just as good as theirs? Look at all the business they have."

I assured Susan that her brochure was fine and that it was every bit as good as those of her potential competitors. But I didn't think any of the brochures—hers or her competition's—were particularly effective direct marketing tools.

Each of the brochures focused on what the company did. As such they were good "business plans." They were like "menus" which told all about the services they provided and how well they provided them. Some even included lists of satisfied customers. What was missing from the brochures was the <u>customer's viewpoint</u>. What benefits would the potential client derive from their services? Why should they use these companies?

Seeing a business from a customer's viewpoint is not easy. Most owners are proud of what they do and how they do it. They are steeped in the features that they offer—but features and benefits are not the same.

For example, in Susan's case the fact that she has experience in developing computer systems to administer employee benefits is an attractive feature of her business. But from a customer viewpoint it would be better to point out that a client could have a system that will keep more accurate records for less money, without having to hire permanent staff to develop it.

I advised Susan to think through each of her services and to identify what it would mean to her customer—the best outcome from the client's point of view. Would the client save money or have more loyal, productive employees? What results could a client expect from Susan's efforts?

The more marketing focuses you have the more difficult your marketing will be

Because Susan can provide a number of consulting services, it's necessary to decide which of these services the marketing should be focused on.

"I don't understand," Susan objected, "why I shouldn't cover all my services. I'll lose business if I don't tell my clients what I do. They won't know all my capabilities, and they may go to another consultant."

I understood Susan's reasoning. When marketing to

existing prospective clients who have already decided to use your services, you need to make them aware of all the "features" you offer. The best business growth is often achieved, particularly in a field like Susan's, by doing an increasing amount of consulting with clients who already know and trust you.

That is not Susan's situation at this time, however. She has no clients. She must convince the first "somebody" to be her client. And the general rule is: The narrower the marketing focus, the stronger your marketing will be.

Let's look at examples of narrowing the marketing focus. In Susan's case, the size and sophistication of each client may dictate how narrow the focus needs to be. For a small business client, just being an "employee benefits consultant" is probably a sufficiently narrow focus, because no one in the company will specialize in employee benefits. A small business would be attracted to the idea of a consultant to ensure they have the best plans for the least money.

In a medium-sized business, there is probably a full time staff member who specializes in employee benefits. Susan could be a consultant who does computer system development for employee benefits. That would be an appropriate focus. The medium-sized company would be lured by the notion of more accurate records and less administrative cost.

A very large company will have a full-time staff specializing in employee benefits. In such a case, what could Susan offer to someone who has never heard of her that would inspire setting up a meeting with her? The focus here needs to be narrow. Susan had developed an "on line" computer system that employees could use to discover and even calculate their own benefits. A large company could be convinced that such a system would improve employee knowledge of benefits and, therefore, loyalty to the company. It would also save existing staff time.

Obviously Susan's business is much broader than an "on line" computer system to explain benefits to employees. Assuming that it's a timely and worthwhile idea, will this narrow a marketing focus hurt Susan's marketing or help it? This approach should make her marketing much easier. It may be exactly the specific focus she needs in order to stand a chance of breaking into larger companies that she is approaching "cold." Smaller companies may also perceive of it as a good idea. They may want to explore it, and that opens the door for other services they may need even more.

"I'm beginning to understand," said Susan. "I can see that when I was sitting in the big corporation I would have been more attracted by a mailing focused on a very specific subject. We would have assumed that a general service was something we could do just as well ourselves, whether we actually could or not.

"But," continued Susan, "couldn't I also add that I successfully implemented this new savings plan under the Internal Revenue Code? Isn't that a valid focus? Not many companies have done that yet."

I told Susan that the Savings Plan might be a good focus, but to be most effective it should be used by itself. The more marketing focuses that you have the more difficult your marketing.

"Yes, but..." said Susan, in frustration.

(Making the leap from a company viewpoint to a customer's viewpoint is difficult for many business owners. However, it is far more difficult to deal with the lack of sales that results from not making the leap.)

**A strong marketing focus creates
endless opportunities to open
doors and create new business—
Cindy Sorrento**

A solid marketing focus is a sure sign of a successful business. Cindy's clients are well identified. They are families that place a high value on belongings and don't want them wrecked by a mover.

The high quality service that she offers is now giving Cindy many opportunities to estimate jobs. Word of mouth referrals are commonplace. It's also the best kind of business in that it will grow steadily over the years. "If I'm so successful, how come I'm not making enough money?" Cindy complained.

Cindy needs to build her business faster. She must find more of her clients—those who place high value on their belongings. Cindy concentrates her marketing efforts on wealthy neighborhoods. It's both logical and a lesson she learned the hard way. She can attract lots of estimates in middle-income neighborhoods, but it's usually a waste of time because they end up using her lower-priced competitors.

Cindy has built most of her business through personal contacts. Her charm, beauty, and her background as an entertainer have all helped her to associate with wealthy people. How can she reach more of them?

One logical and very effective marketing strategy is to go to the next level by reaching the professionals who deal with your potential customers. Cindy can increase her business by establishing more professional referrals. Who sells her clients their homes? Who decorates their homes? Who sells them furniture?

Cindy already knew some of these crucial people, and her concentrated efforts proved to be rewarding. It started to produce a network of the best kind of referrals—cross referrals. Cindy had many opportunities to refer her clients to real estate brokers and interior decorators. They returned the favor.

As a result of these efforts, Cindy also started getting some commercial deliveries from a furniture store. This introduced the idea of a commercial moving business as a secondary market focus—a long range possibility for Cindy.

(A strong marketing focus creates endless opportunities—it opens doors and creates new business.)

Who are your customers? — introducing "Over the Transom Marketing"

I often wonder what would have happened if someone had come into my law school class and asked, "How many would like to be bankruptcy lawyers? Raise your hands. How many would like to be divorce lawyers? Hands up." My guess is that no hands would have been raised. But handling divorce and bankruptcy are what most of those former students do for a living today.

I might add that most lawyers are not completely happy with the direction their businesses have taken. It isn't really what they had in mind. Then why did they allow it to happen? Many lawyers start their private practice much as I did—sitting in my office, doing crossword puzzles while waiting for clients to call. After all, active marketing was not professional, or even ethical, in those days, and working crossword puzzles was a respectable intellectual pursuit.

What saved me was that most of the clients walking through my door were interested in real estate transactions. I found that so dull that I went back to the corporation. Most of my former colleagues were luckier. Eventually a juicy bankruptcy or divorce case walked through their doors and they did a super job on it, so good a job that referrals to similar cases catapulted them into lucrative practices. Eventually they became specialists in something they weren't much interested in to begin with. I call the marketing that leads to these results, "over the transom marketing." You sit there and accept whatever comes through the door. In other words, you have lost control of your marketing and your business.

A strong benefit can create its own marketing focus — the "Greasy Spoon" that turned to gold

This is the story of a "greasy spoon" restaurant. They might call them diners or coffee shops in your area, but I know they exist in every nook and cranny of the country. You can spot them by their plastic-coated menus offering dozens of dishes ranging from the mundane burger to exotic Hawaiian chicken. One glance at the menu and you know you're in trouble. These places are good for breakfast, but for other meals they may start with basically good food, but they figure out a way to ruin it.

This is the story of a greasy spoon that had a bit of luck. Friends of mine happened upon it and suggested I give it a try. So one evening when I was taking the love of my life out to dinner, I headed for the greasy spoon. When we got to the front door of the place she balked, "I'm not going into that dump!" I told her that at least three friends had told me it had the greatest food ever.

The owner by accident or marriage had recently acquired a gourmet cook. In a "stroke of genius," as it turned out, the owner decided to list everything that the gourmet cook prepared on a yellow insert attached to the menu. No other marketing was done.

Finally after promising we would leave if she wasn't comfortable, we entered. It was great food, and we went back many times.

In time the "greasy spoon" added two additional dining rooms and tripled in size. However, I ate there recently and tried something that wasn't on the yellow insert—a big mistake. I had indigestion for a week. Underneath that yellow insert the greasy spoon still lives!

Would this approach be a good marketing focus for Alex to adopt for his restaurant? It was taking the simple straight forward view that if the customers got great food, they would come back. I suggested this to Alex and he has tried some of his favorite dishes on a special insert.

(Both Alex and I thought it would work. It hasn't yet, mainly, I think, because Alex is unable to focus as much on cooking as he needs to or would like to.)

The more ideas you have the more likely you are to have a marketing problem

I've had the opportunity to work with at least six clients whom I consider to be geniuses. Each of these clients has had streaks of brilliant success but none have the consistently successful business they should have. The common thread in these cases is too many good ideas. Before one good idea can be fully implemented, they are rushing off to get another one started.

Lack of marketing focus usually causes the breakdown in the business. A consistently successful business carefully identifies its customer and works on understanding the customer viewpoint. Too many ideas can create too many types of customers, and maintaining the customer viewpoint on each becomes increasingly difficult. Stated another way, the more ideas you have the more likely you are to have a marketing problem.

Who is the customer? How will I reach the customer?

Bob and Dolores have a potential problem in their growth planning because they have so many directions from which to choose.

A logical way to sort out each focus is to analyze: "Who is the customer?" and "How will I reach the customer?" If each focus means a different set of customers, then there is a loss of focus, and marketing efforts will be diluted. Unless you have unlimited resources that can be applied to marketing, this can spell disaster.

The original focus of the business was "gifts." In order to smooth out the seasonal nature of the gift business, Bob and Dolores added office supplies. Although the office supply business has been successful, it has become more competitive and it has diluted the overall marketing effort.

Bob and Dolores believe that greeting cards are the core of the business. Dolores, in particular, is very comfortable in the gift business and believes that it is what they do best.

"Since most of our customers perceive us as a gift shop," said Dolores, "isn't that the direction we should go? There are numerous ways we could expand our gift lines."

"I don't see how we can drop office supplies," replied Bob. "This store could get lonely in the non- holiday months if we dropped office supplies."

Actually, Bob and Dolores are both right. A decision is often based on timing, current situations, and goals. When they added office supplies, their business was a lot smaller than it is now. An added profit center that provided stable income between gift-buying seasons was a good decision. Now Bob and Dolores have a larger and more profitable store. Furthermore, they want to expand in a relatively short time to meet their retirement goals.

Expanding office supplies would require going out and increasing the customer base and perhaps moving into a new field such as selling and servicing office equipment. They have a base to start from and there is good potential, but it would take time and energy to do it.

Expanding the gift business would mean adding additional card and book lines. They would be selling more to their existing customers—and it appears that their customers would welcome the opportunity to buy more from them.

Bob and Dolores needed to decide whether they could build the gift-season business enough to more than offset the stable office supply. They decided that they could. The key to their decision was their customers' perception that they were a gift shop.

(This decision was based on a need for <u>growth</u> rather than <u>survival.</u> This was a change in thinking for Bob and Dolores. It's the kind of change every owner needs to make to develop a really successful business.)

The problem of reaching your customer. Thank goodness Tom Edison finally found a backer for his light bulb

Mike and Jim have always had a good sense of their ultimate customer's viewpoint. But they have never fully realized just who their customer is.

They actually enjoy playing the games they manufacture. So do I. We have a wonderful sense about the games big kids (and small kids, too) love to play. Mike and Jim have created so much fun for people in the last ten years, they should qualify for a Nobel prize.

The problem is that kids are not their customers. Distributors and large retailers are their customers. And from the viewpoint of these potential customers, Mike and Jim are not valuable suppliers because they are not "full line" manufacturers.

Mr. Retailer, their major customer, is so large that he can purchase huge quantities of even one or two games and he does consider Mike and Jim profitable suppliers. The attitude most other distributors take is that they might be interested in doing business if more games were offered, but otherwise it's not worth their time.

Coming up with more games to fill out a line is harder than it sounds. Each game should be a proven good seller and development and market testing is very expensive. Mike and Jim are not inclined to expand their line unless they find just the right combination.

The problem of finding distribution channels is not unique to Mike and Jim. Virtually every new product needs a distribution channel to be successful.

We can only speculate on how many products of real merit have failed because a way to distribute then couldn't be found. (Thank goodness Tom Edison ultimately found a backer for his light bulb.) Still, Mike and Jim need to diversify. If Mr. Retailer decided to change how he buys product lines, Mike and Jim would be out in the cold.

The statistical baseball game was rejected by Mr. Retailer and other distributors, but it could be the key to diversifying the business. The big advantage of the mail order approach is that for once Mike and Jim will know their customers' viewpoint, because the customers are the "big and small kids" and not the distributors.

(Mike and Jim are quite intrigued with the idea of a mail order business. They find they have a new sense of control over the business which they have been lacking for years.)

As you have seen, asking the simple question, "Who is our customer?", goes a long way toward moving a business in the right direction. Targeting and understanding the business from your customer's view will make your marketing much easier.

In most retail businesses a location decision probably is the most important an owner will make. It has many implications in other types of businesses as well. In the next chapter we'll take a look at what causes bad location decisions.

CHAPTER FIVE

The Location Decision: Is There Anything More Important Than Location?

A bad location is a big problem

When one is seeking to define a good retail location, being close to a busy restaurant is part of that definition. People eat all the time: food attracts a crowd.

However, just opening a restaurant doesn't mean that you are in a good location. The most vivid example I can recall was the family restaurant that was in plain view of 50,000 cars every day. The only problem was that the cars were going 55 miles an hour and there was no direct access to the restaurant parking lot. A patron had to go down a side road and come in from behind the restaurant.

This was a small business with a big marketing prob-

"Perhaps you can find a comfortable
office from which to run your business."

lem. Two high powered marketing consultants had done some brilliant work but revenues were still too low. The answer was painfully simple. If part of the curb were removed so that there was direct access to the parking lot, the restaurant would have been highly successful. At least that was my opinion.

The government refused to allow the curb removal. The best solution was for the owner to take a sledge hammer, go out in the middle of the night, remove the curb, and take his chances in court. Actually, the owner was stuck with his choice of court appearances. It was either fight the curb in court or end up in bankruptcy court. He chose to continue to try and market the restaurant with the curb in place and, in fact, ended up in bankruptcy court.

Advertising, public relations, and other forms of marketing can be very effective tools to increase business, but if you have to overcome a bad location, you had better have very deep pockets. I don't think trying to overcome a bad location makes sense in most cases. I have refused to work with a number of clients unless they changed locations. In fact, location is so important that trying to overcome a bad location isn't something I am willing to spend any time doing.

A home-based business can make sense

When she worked in the corporation, Susan had an office on the 50th floor which commanded a view of half the city. On a clear day she could see the sand dunes across Lake Michigan. Susan is experiencing something of a culture shock because now her office is her kitchen table and she has a clear view of the garbage cans.

"Do I need an office?", Susan asked. "Most of my work will be done at my client's site. The only problem is that I'm having trouble getting going in the morning."

Dr. Wright to the rescue! I'm full of ideas on how to get going in the morning. I eagerly explained my program of taking an hour's walk before breakfast every day. It supplies my aerobic points and gives me strong legs and tough calluses on my feet. (I must admit that it hasn't done much for my pot belly.)

Like most of my clients, Susan listened patiently as I argued the virtues of a morning walk, but she didn't appear enthusiastic about leaping out of bed at 5 a.m. on a cold winter morning. Oh well. All I can do is advise.

The idea of having a business at home appeals to many people. Sometimes I think that half the homes in the country have a business operating in them. Many of the zoning laws forbid having a business in the home, which probably makes home based business one of the major illegal activities in the nation.

Generally I support the zoning laws. The idea of signs and crowds of shoppers in a residential area is not appealing, nor does it make for good business in most cases. Enforcement of these laws is generally focused on those businesses that become a nuisance to the neighbors. That seems reasonable and probably saves the laws from being repealed.

There are other issues about operating a business out of the home that Susan should consider. They involve Susan's self-image and also the image that she projects to others.

The image created by having a home-based business is often that of a non-serious business. And it is true that many home-based businesses are not committed and not serious.

But commitment is based on the owner's state of mind, regardless of location.

There are obvious advantages to Susan having her business in her home. She will save time and money. If Susan can be effective working out of her home, then she should do it. It's a matter of her attitude. If Susan feels she can't be effective unless she establishes an outside office, then she should start looking for an office.

An office for Susan could be more than just a place to work. Susan could choose an office in a bank, insurance company, actuarial firm, or any other company whose services would complement hers. This would set up a very likely possibility of cross referrals. It could become an important part of her marketing.

Another consideration is the impression which Susan's address will make on her clients. Will Susan's home address properly convey the high-powered experienced person that Susan is? If other employee benefits consultants are located on a major street, isn't that where Susan should be too?

Don't under estimate the importance of the location decision in any business. It has an impact on more areas of your business than you'd expect.

(Susan started her business from home but also set up a mailing address and office use privileges at a downtown location. Sometimes she complains of being lonely working at home and so it wouldn't surprise me to see her locate in an office with other consultants in the near future.)

The thrill of a home based business —
introducing Sabre

I like to use my living room as an office to see clients. I have always felt that it was important to get small business owners out of their normal surroundings so they can more easily focus on the future. This has worked very well for many years, but it is subject to normal household interruptions such as people who want to read meters or collect for charity.

The most "exciting" day I ever spent working at home happened because of one of these ordinary household interruptions. My large red haired kitty named "Sabre" enjoys the freedom of going outside and coming back inside at will. Sabre has me so well trained that I will frequently let him in or out without even interrupting my conversation with a client.

Almost unconsciously I had let Sabre in, when my client paused and said in a very calm voice, "Hal, your cat just brought in a mouse." I looked to the other side of the room and saw Sabre playing with a mouse. This was hardly the proper atmosphere for a serious consultation. I went and got a broom but Sabre was too quick and he raced upstairs with his mouse. So I sat down and resumed the consultation holding my broom in hand.

Oh, the joys of a home based office! So as not to leave you in suspense, eventually Sabre came back downstairs still holding his prize. They got between me and the door and I was able to sweep them both out. I often wonder what would have happened if I had been working with one of my more excitable clients at the time.

The case of the extra loud telephone

I was meeting with a prospective client for the first time when I heard a horn honking. The client jumped out of his chair and raced out of my office to his car. He returned in a short time and explained to me that he had his car phone hooked up to his horn. In the next hour the horn was to honk three more times and each time a mad dash ensued. By the time he returned for the third time, I was laughing so hard I couldn't continue the meeting.

I never did work with that client but an associate of mine did. My associate was to meet him at a restaurant one day. When my associate arrived at the address he could find no restaurant. He called but got no answer. He drove around and came to a restaurant at a different address. On going in he found his client fuming, "Where have you been? Why didn't you call?"

My associate responded that he did call, but the client shouted, "That's a lie, the horn never honked." The client then went to a pay phone and dialed his number and there was no honk. When last seen he was under the hood trying to get it rigged up again.

This new communication age that we live in has redefined where a small business owner has to be to run the business. Thank goodness the carphone/horn combination hasn't caught on. But many other devices have become the normal way to do business. Cindy is a good case in point. For all practical purposes Cindy's primary office is her car.

The location could be where ever you are

Cindy rents an office in a furniture storage ware-house. She has a desk in a garage where her trucks are stored and maintained. She also has an office in her home. But most of Cindy's day is spent in her car because she is out making estimates or is at a moving job.

By using a carphone, a beeper, a computer, a FAX machine, an answering machine, and an answering service, Cindy is able to maximize the time she spends marketing and supervising, which are her primary roles. Cindy's real loca-tion should be in her clients' homes and by using all these techniques she is able to be where she should be most of the time.

(The location of Cindy's business can truly be defined as wherever she is.)

You must know where your customers live and work

The role of location in the marketing of a professional practice may be just as important as it is for a retail store, but it is not as obvious and it's much harder to evaluate. Some years ago I was working with a medical practice that was about six years old and had never grown as the doctors had hoped. We had improved their marketing techniques, and one day I asked the doctors how many of their patients could walk to their office. In other words, how many of their patients either lived or worked within 3 or 4 blocks of the office.

They couldn't answer my question so they reviewed their records. It turned out that just a small number of patients fit that description, despite the fact that the doctors had spent time getting to know their neighbors and were visible in the community.

Within the next six months, they moved their office to an area where they had a heavier concentration of patients. Six months after the move the practice had doubled. We don't really know for sure what was wrong with the previous location. But the doctors had spent six years proving it was wrong. If one has a professional practice which serves the general public, a good percentage of the patients or clients should come from the area where the practice is located.

A location can change with the time of day

In Alex's case, I identified the location as a problem of the business. Alex is on a busy street, but is about two blocks away from "heaven."

Two blocks away is where the action is. There is extensive street traffic and a cluster of other restaurants. Common sense would dictate that Alex should relocate to get the advantage of this heavier traffic. This is a common phenomenon in which a "restaurant row" draws patrons to the area. It is much easier to compete with the restaurant next door than it is to train people to walk an extra two blocks.

However, moving is out of the question at this time. Current financial conditions and a past credit history made it impossible for Alex to move now.

The process of making a business more successful

includes constantly testing the facts to make better decisions, and it's usually a process that is done with planning over time. On occasion, however, there is a dramatic break-through and this is what happened in Alex's case. I've often said "It is better to be lucky than good."

Alex's restaurant is located about 20 miles from me and I very seldom get into that area. One night I was invited to a party in that suburb. On the way back home, I mentioned to my friends that I had a restaurant client in town and drove by to show them where it was. It was about midnight as we passed by the darkened restaurant. To my amazement, there were throngs of people on the street in front of the restaurant and in the general area. The source of this crowd was readily apparent. There was a movie theater about a block away, and Alex was located on the street between the movie theater and the major parking area.

Most of my childhood was before the arrival of television so I can relate to the days when everyone went to a movie once a week. For most of my adult life, however, I've regarded movie houses as businesses with a big competitive problem or as I might call it, a "dinosaur" or "buggy whip" business.

A new trend has now taken hold which apparently has changed the economics of the movie business. The big auditoriums have been broken up into three or four theatres and the prices have been lowered. The result is that movie houses, or at least the one down the street from Alex, are now drawing crowds.

In a very real sense, Alex has two "locations", or perhaps even three locations, depending on the time of day. There is the early morning-going-to-work-breakfast crowd. Then there is the non-crowd afternoon and early evening.

Now there appears to be a late evening after-the-movie crowd.

Alex is closed at the very time that his location might be at its best. Initially, Alex was somewhat negative about my suggestion that he test the movie crowd market. He told me how he had thought about it before and how it probably wouldn't work. I think these answers were a product of his fatigue.

I asked Alex if he had been around the restaurant between 9 p.m and midnight lately. When he said that he hadn't, I suggested that he drive over and see what's happening—just to appease me.

Alex did visit the restaurant that night and the next week he extended his store hours to midnight.

(Alex is now working to build his after-the-movie business up to the level of his breakfast business. He has discovered a <u>new</u> value in his <u>old</u> location.)

How to avoid choosing a bad location

When you advise other people, it is easy to fall into the trap of beginning to believe that you can overcome any problem. I try hard to avoid this trap, and I've become pretty successful at avoiding the really bad locations.

If a business that is trying to cater to the public opens up in a bad location, it will be at a severe marketing disadvantage. The money that is spent in "catch-up" advertising will be many times the rent "saved" in the new location. My files are full of disastrous location decisions. There was the hidden convenience store and the sports center on a deadend street that could only be seen from a moving train. Whenever I meet a prospective client in such a pickle, I advise them to either "move it or close it." Bad location is usually not an "overcomeable" problem.

Bob and Dolores have a great location. It's the foundation of their successful business. But I've learned more about the psychology behind bad location decisions in working with Bob and Dolores than through any other source.

For the last year Bob and Dolores have been looking to open a second location. The planning and the financing are in place. All that is needed is the right location.

Location is unique. If another business is occupying the "right" location it's not available for you. Just because you are ready to locate, there is no law that requires a good location to be available.

Opening a business involves a lot of emotional decisions. It's an act of courage as well as logic. On three different occasions in the last year, I've had to throw cold water on one of Bob and Dolores' choice for a second location.

In each situation Bob and Dolores were ready to commit to a second location that had a major flaw (usually lack of traffic). They had talked themselves into these situations by accentuating the positive to the point that they stopped noticing the major flaw which was always obvious.

It didn't take much to talk them out of all three locations. Usually I asked cute little questions or made statements like, "How will your customers find you?", or "At least there is a lot of parking."

So anyone looking for a retail location, beware! Beware of your own impatience. It can fog your mind. It can get you into a situation where you can't succeed and no one can help you. It happens every day. Don't let it happen to you.

(There is a secondary reason why some people choose a bad location. That is ego. They may believe that they are so talented they can overcome everything, even bad location.)

"Where It's Made" does make a difference

Can a small manufacturer survive in the United States today? I suppose the answer depends on what is manufactured.

In today's global economy this is a very real day to day issue to a business like Mike and Jim's. They believe their profits have been squeezed by foreign competition. If they are squeezed any harder, Mike and Jim will be forced to stop manufacturing in the United States. The only way they will be able to stay in business is to have their games manufactured overseas and become distributors. For many reasons, they don't want to do that.

(Is location important to a manufacturer? Where were your car and your television set made?)

"Don't tell them the price until
they understand the benefits."

CHAPTER SIX

Pricing: Will My Customers Pay What I Need to Charge?

The customer's perception of value is usually the most important factor in determining price — Introducing "The Jerk Level."

If there is such a thing as a "universal moment of truth" to a small business owner, it is at the time when pricing decisions are made.

Making a good pricing decision is a lot harder than it looks. At first glance, it doesn't appear to be much of a problem. You know your price has to cover your costs and allow for your profit. If your price is in line with your competition, then your decision is made. Right?

It's seldom that easy because price is directly related to many other factors of the business. Overhead, volume, and capacity are part of every pricing decision.

I know many business owners who are much more comfortable in a period of inflation, mainly because they feel there is less risk in a decision to increase prices. The effects of bad pricing decisions are often hard to determine because customers may not react immediately. The key factor is the perceived value of your goods or services in your customers' eyes. Any techniques that you can use to show greater value will entitle you to a higher price.

This story is about a young man who was laid off from his factory job. He had always been rather handy and so he decided to start a home handyman service. A little advertising generated many calls and he was on his way. As he visited these potential customers, he looked at the work to be done and estimated the time he would need to do it. When asked how much he charged, he said $10 per hour, because that was how much he had been making at his factory job.

The reaction of most of his potential customers was immediate. Ten dollars per hour! How wonderful! In fact, about nine out of ten of his customers readily agreed and asked how soon he could get started.

However, one in ten of this young man's prospective customers would quibble about his price. Now this lad had never taken the course on winning friends and influencing people. He was quite outspoken and somewhat crude in his language. But he had a ready response when his price was questioned. He said to himself or, depending on his mood, out loud, "YOU JERK," and then he walked out.

As you can guess, since nine out of ten potential customers were happy with his price, his business grew rapidly and he decided to change his price to $15 per hour. Most of his customers still quickly agreed and asked how soon he could get started. But now, about two out of ten people quibbled over his price. When that happened, he again responded, "YOU JERK." and he walked out.

What we began to realize was that as he increased his prices, he was increasing THE JERK LEVEL. Perhaps at $25 per hour, half of his prospects would be jerks. At $100 per hour, they might all be jerks!

We were about to test the $20 per hour level when my young friend was recalled to his factory job and he terminated his business. (Not everyone has a burning desire to be an entrepreneur.) However, my outspoken friend with his short-lived business taught me a valuable lesson which I have shared many times.

There is a JERK LEVEL in every business. Pricing is an art. Your pricing must hit a balance to be acceptable to both your customers and yourself, in order to provide the profit margins you need to have a successful business.

The lesson here is not that it is okay to call those who don't like your price "jerks." If you own a small business, you need to win friends and influence people and this is seldom appropriate as a sales tactic.

I know a lot of you are thinking about prospective customers who you believe really were jerks. No matter how you set your prices, they objected to them. But were they really jerks? Think about it.

Yes, there is a lunatic fringe who will object to anything. Yes, there are "pretend" buyers who are not really qualified to buy what you are selling. But I believe that very often we help to create jerks out of prospective customers.

Unless buyers understand the benefit of what they are buying, <u>any price</u> is too much. It is too easy to over emphasize price as the key element of a sales transaction. Often it is not.

Let's go back to the example of our home handyman. You will recall that he responded to each inquiry by going to the prospective client's home and looking at the work to be done. He was obviously creating the impression that he could do the work. Suppose he had simply sat with his telephone and quoted a $10 per hour price without going out to actually see the project. Would 9 out of 10 callers have agreed to have him get started? The answer, of course, is no. He tried it. It didn't work at all. They were all "jerks." That's why he went out to look at the work.

Whenever potential customers object to your price, you'd better find out if they understood the benefits. A key part of your sales process is to make sure your customer fully understands the value of what you do.

You had better understand your customers' needs and educate them about how you are going to meet those needs, before you ever mention price. If you don't do that, any price might be too much and you may make "jerks" out of those who could have been your most valuable customers.

The 1/3 rule of thumb for service businesses

I was working late one night and was about ready to call it a day when the phone rang. It was Susan Andrews, the employee benefits consultant.

"Oh, Hal, I have good, good news. A client just agreed to a $20,000 project. I did what you told me to do, and it all worked! It's going to be a great project. These are wonderful clients."

I was very excited by Susan's news, and I thanked her for telling me about it. But, I was also a little embarrassed. It was late, I was tired, and I had a mental gap. I was having trouble remembering the particular advice I had given her that had caused this happy result.

Susan had made a number of good marketing decisions and had created a lot of prospects. Unfortunately, she was having trouble closing sales. One reason for this problem was her discomfort at having to price her services at $100 per hour.

After all, $100 x 40 hours x 52 weeks is $208,000 a year. She had been comfortable with her $60,000 per year salary in the corporation. Why should she charge so much?

Part of the answer is that the owners of consulting and professional practices find it very difficult to consistently bill more than twenty hours per week, mainly because of the time required for marketing and administration.

Another part of the answer is the rule of thumb that says you should allot 1/3 of your hourly rate to cover overhead such as rent, utilities, secretarial help and marketing services. This can be controlled but it is a realistic percentage in many situations. This means that $33 of the $100 rate is allocated to overhead, leaving only $67 to pay Susan.

Also, 52 weeks of work is unrealistic when vacation, sick days, and holidays are considered. Forty-eight weeks per year is more like it. So the more realistic calculation is $67 x 20 hours x 48 weeks = $64,320. That is why $100 per hour rate is necessary to sustain a $60,000 per year income for Susan.

"I agree with the numbers. I do need to charge $100 per hour, but every time I try to tell a client that price it gets stuck in my throat. I feel like a robber-baron," said Susan. "Do you realize that $100 per hour is $1.66 per minute? My clients will be afraid to ask me how the weather is for fear it will cost $5.00 for me to tell them."

"Actually, if the $100 makes you uncomfortable, you may want to change it to $95," I said. "That does sound like a lot less."

When inflation was pushing up prices like crazy, many professionals and senior consultants stopped at $95 per hour for a long time because they felt that $100 was a psychological barrier. When they did increase their fees, many jumped from $95 to $125 per hour figuring once the barrier was broken, they had better make sure that they were compensated.

Nevertheless, your hourly rate should never become the big issue. The issue should be the value you are going to create for your customers.

When what you do changes, you must change the price for what you do — introducing the L.A. Caper

Let's look at the $20,000 project Susan sold. During her next visit Susan told me she was going to work on some changes in this company's insurance administration. Her work should save the company about $120,000 a year. Now that's creating value! But I asked Susan how she arrived at her price. Was it just an estimate subject to actual hours, or was the $20,000 a fixed amount?

Susan told me that she'd estimated research, writing, and meeting time at each stage of the project. A number of departments were going to be involved and the entire budget was about $150,000. Susan's role was to spearhead the project and work closely with the Benefits Manager. She had run a similar project while in her corporate job and was confident about her estimates. She thought the project would take about 10 hours per week for 20 weeks, hence $20,000.

"But," I asked, "are you at risk if the project takes longer? In other words, if you spend more than 200 hours of your time can you charge more?"

She said she was locked in to the price, but she was confident enough about the time not to be worried. This left me to worry for her. "Susan," I said, "your problems have just begun. You need to realize that clients change their minds in the middle of projects and this affects you."

It was time to tell Susan another story. This particular escapade I call the L.A. Caper. One of my clients was given the opportunity to bid on a film production for a large company. Much like Susan, he'd had experience with similar projects while employed in a corporation and he identified each piece of the project and came up with a good time estimate.

I reviewed the proposal with my client before he submitted it, and I suggested he double his estimate. I had a couple of good reasons. First, much of his time was going to be under the control of the client company. The client had also demanded a fixed bid—a fixed price. I knew he had better allow for extra meetings and delays over which he would have little control.

My client agreed to go along with my advice, he doubled the bid and won the job. But, several months later he walked into my office looking as if he'd been run over by a tank. His mood matched his appearance.

"Remember the film project?" he said. "Well, I've put so much time into it, and it's turned into a loser. And I can't even bill for all of it."

He started giving the gory details. At first things seemed fine. Scripts were approved and local shooting took place. "But the time really expanded," he said, "when we went to Los Angeles."

"Hold everything," I said. "This is the first time I've heard about a trip to Los Angeles. That wasn't part of the proposal."

It seems that the idea to shoot some footage in L. A. came up long after production started. Actually, it was a good idea and improved the film. But, from my client's perspective, it was disastrous. More film was shot than planned— enough for two more films. But his editing time had increased far beyond his original estimate.

I asked my client if he had raised the problem of his increased time and other costs with the project manager.

"No," he said. "I assumed he was taking that time into consideration."

I don't think an outside consultant can <u>ever</u> assume that a client is aware of the costs when projects change. The consultant <u>must</u> raise the cost issue and submit a new estimate.

In the case of the "L. A. Caper" we separated the costs of the trip and the increased editing. Actually, if you eliminated the cost of the Los Angeles shoot, the original estimate had worked out as we had planned. (It should be noted that doubling his estimate turned out to be absolutely necessary!)

We decided to submit two separate bills. One bill was for the project as originally proposed. The other covered the costs related to the Los Angeles part of the project. It worked and the company paid both bills.

However, there is a downside to this story. My client didn't receive any more film producing contracts from that company. All the company could see was that the film had run far over budget. My client might have prevented that problem if he had raised the cost issue at the time the decision to go to L. A. had been made, and had it approved by "higher-ups" in the company.

"So Susan, what is the moral of the story?"

"Never go to Los Angeles with a film crew?" laughed Susan. "Seriously, I guess you are trying to tell me that I need to keep my pricing hat on all through the big project to keep my client on track. If I don't, I'm the one who will suffer in the long run."

Beautifully put!

(Ultimately, Susan's insurance project dragged on for a year because her client company kept on changing its mind. However, because she kept raising the cost issue, she received $35,000 for this project and her client was as happy as could be.)

A high-priced service must find its unique market

Cindy is a good one to test the "jerk level" theory because she knows that everyone will not be her customer. The moving business is highly regulated. It requires special licenses and price rates must be filed with state commissions. Cindy's rates are at the high end of the scale because she aims at the upscale, wealthy market. Her service level matches her price.

When Cindy goes into a home to estimate a job she is dressed in fashionable designer clothing. Her three inch heels add to the image of an upscale company executive. It's obvious that this petite little charmer wouldn't have the strength to pick up an ashtray. By the time she finishes her estimate most customers are convinced that her company will move their valuables more safely and efficiently than anyone else.

Cindy's estimates are often far higher than her competition's estimates but she projects the value she gives. The customer "jerk level" is based on how much they value their belongings and how well they are convinced that she will preserve them.

Her pricing is based on the time and number of men required to do the job, and her estimates always include one extra man so that no crew is ever rushed. Preparation and clean up can be done carefully.

There is a "rule of thumb" that states that for a service business to be profitable, the hourly rate must be at least three times the hourly cost of labor. Cindy sets her prices at four times the rate she pays for labor so that business can be profitable.

The moving business is highly competitive and price is often an issue. Cindy is always torn between maintaining her quality and charging her price but she wonders how much business she is losing because of her high prices.

Cindy and I decided to track the percentage of estimates that were accepted. Fortunately, Cindy is very efficient and she had a written estimate for each job going back two years.

Cindy brought her analysis to our next session and it revealed an interesting pattern. Three years earlier she had been getting business on 20 to 25% of the estimates she had been making. Over time, this number had been shrinking until she was currently getting the job on only 10% to 15% of her estimates. Ironically, the number of estimates she was giving had doubled so that her overall business had increased, but not by much.

When you state the price is often as important as the price you state

I was convinced that Cindy could improve her percentages. I asked her to show me the process she used to work up her estimate. Basically, she went through the prospect's house, asking all the important questions about the goods being moved, and taking notes. Then she went back to her office to work out the figures, following up with a phone call and a letter to confirm the estimate.

I asked Cindy if she could give an estimate on the spot, to increase the probability of closing the sale. "No," she said. "I'd run the risk of underestimating the job and losing money or overestimating it and losing the move."

It was time for me to share another story to illustrate an important point.

When I was young and working my way up in the corporation, I had a boss who was really something special. He had super judgement, was excellent in dealing with people, and over the years he had built a reputation as being "Mr. Personnel" in the corporation. However, he had one problem. He was not focused on detail, particularly the level of detail in the company personnel plans.

On a day to day basis he was vulnerable to all kinds of questions about company policies asked by any employee at any time. He soon realized that if he responded to these questions by saying truthfully, "I don't know" or "I'm not sure," his reputation would be adversely affected. After all, if "Mr. Personnel" didn't know the answer, then who would? So he was forced to give the best answer that he could.

Once he gave that answer, his priorities changed. He would need to race back to his office to verify the answer he had given. I would see my boss returning from the bathroom and he'd growl at me, "Wright, get into my office." I'd think, oh my gosh, what have I done now? Once we were seated, he usually started by saying, "I just ran into so-and-so in the hall and they asked me about such-and-such and I told them so-and-so. How does that sound?"

If I said that sounded okay, he would be pleased and we'd talk about other business or the Cubs or golf. If I questioned the response, we would discuss it and he would be on the phone saying, "Oh, Charlie, remember we just had that conversation in the hall. I forgot to ask you...." As you can see, he was a credible person who deserved to be called "Mr. Personnel".

Let's apply that to small business. Suppose you wanted a couple of new electrical outlets and a ceiling fan installed in your home and you called an electrician for an estimate. The electrician comes out and looks around and says that he will work up an estimate and send it to you. What would you think?

Cindy thought, and I imagine you feel the same way, that the electrician must be a rookie. But, let's give him the benefit of the doubt. House wiring systems vary depending on when they were installed. The electrician may have had to do considerable research to find the costs of certain parts. But this is not apparent to you, the customer.

When you cannot give your potential customer a price on the spot, you lose some credibility. The longer it takes you to give a price, the more credibility you lose. Yet there can be no sale until the price is known. Cindy was losing sales because of this.

Cindy agreed and said, "On 90% of the estimates, I know within a few dollars what the move will cost. I'll start giving my best estimate immediately, to be verified in writing within 24 house. I'll close them on the spot contingent upon its accuracy. Then I'll run back to my office to check it out like your former boss did."

If price is a problem, why not give your customer a choice?

"I have another problem," I said to Cindy. Based on closing only 10 to 15% of your estimates, I think you are losing customers on price.

"Look Hal," said Cindy, "we've had this conversation before. My clients are the upscale market. That's where my contacts are, and that's who I'm committed to. And I'm not about to reduce my prices. I couldn't afford to. I'd go out of business."

"I understand that, Cindy," I said. (We had indeed had this conversation before.) "But suppose we approach it in a way that will not increase risk. I know your clients are upscale, but many are still sensitive to price. I don't care how rich they are, they still want the best service for the lowest price."

Cindy wasn't sure what I was proposing, but I came up with a plan to increase her volume. I told her to try offering her clients three choices and educating them about each one. The first choice would be on the low end. It would be comparable to estimates that her large competitors give clients.

The crew would be smaller and the service somewhat "slam bang".

Her second level would be exactly the same as her current plan. But her third level of pricing would be a package including many added services. "You could have their utilities turned off and on," I said. "You could make their beds and brush their teeth—whatever. But it is luxury level commanding top prices. Maybe it's only for the family moving into a million dollar home."

Cindy was intrigued. "That's crazy," she said. "Let's think about the details and see how it would work."

We spent a couple of hours putting together a detailed plan, and Cindy started testing it the next week. That is one of the joys of working with small businesses. No long feasibility studies. The owners don't have that kind of time.

(These ideas proved successful. They turned out to be the crucial decisions at that stage of Cindy's business development. Almost overnight her moving contracts increased from 15% to 30% of the estimates made. Most of her moves continued to be Level 2 moves, which is what she had been doing all along. About 20% of her moves were at the lower level.)

You need to know what your competitors charge

"Alex, how do you determine prices on your menu?"

"Mostly based on what the competition charges," said Alex.

"Who is your competition? Do you ever patronize them?"

"There are a number of restaurants like mine in the area," said Alex, "and also a number of chains. I rarely eat at any of them, but I look at the menus in their windows all the time."

"Did you just hear yourself say what I heard you say?"

"Sounds as if I should be getting out there and looking at what those other people are passing off as 'good food,' doesn't it?," said Alex.

"You bet. I think your homework for the next two weeks might be to eat one meal a day at a competitor's place and see if your stomach survives. By the way, have you developed the food costs for items on your menu?"

Alex responded, "As you probably could guess, no, I haven't. Let me answer your next question before you ask it. When I managed other people's restaurants I did a complete food cost everyday, and I had every item on the menu costed down to the fraction of a penny. So I know how to do it, I just don't do it for myself. I know what my homework is. You're going to see the best food analysis you've ever seen."

A sleeping giant is awakening.

(Alex never did need to change his pricing very much, but doing the investigation required to make pricing decisions was ultimately crucial in discovering new directions which made his business more successful.)

When your competitor is a discounter, you need to fight fire with some well-placed smoke of your own

When Bob and Dolores opened the book store more than ten years ago, there were very few pricing decisions. Both the book and the card business were based on retail list prices established by the publishers. The book store operated on a 40% margin for both books and cards. Office supplies were bought at wholesale and these costs were doubled to determine the retail price. Therefore office supplies had a 50% margin.

Bob and Dolores never had to make many pricing decisions in their first eight years of business. Prices were determined by the manufacturers. This all changed when the first discount bookstore opened up with great fanfare about a mile and a half away. You could identify the date of that opening by looking at Dolores' monthly financial statements. Book sales dropped like a rock.

About six months later a national discount chain store about two miles away started to emphasize office supplies. As Bob and Dolores joke, in a gallows humor way, that if a national discount chain of greeting card shops opens up, their first store will probably be right across the street.

The Rafertys survived by making arrangements to handle text books for a local college and by setting up special discounts with several banks and other local businesses for their office supply needs. This new business, while only carrying a 20% margin, has enabled the Rafertys to maintain some profits and survive the discounters.

Bob and Dolores thought that because they were small they couldn't compete with the big chains on price.

They had always believed their business could survive by stocking quality items and providing good service. However, their after-Christmas sales and the summer sidewalk sales drew very well.

But while their attitudes made a lot of sense, they weren't looking at price from a customer's point of view. Customers are pretty smart. Down deep, most people know they aren't going to get something for nothing. But, on the other hand, they don't like to feel they are being ripped off. And when real price differences are involved, loyalty to a former supplier who has given you quality and service is likely to be on shaky ground.

The reason for the sale is more important than the sale

When competitors are pushing price, an owner has to be very sensitive about pricing policies or customers will think they are being cheated. An effective pricing promotion can outstrip the discounters at their own game. The key to a price promotion is having a strong reason behind the lower price. That's why after-Christmas sales are so effective. Everybody knows you're anxious to get rid of extra stock that you didn't sell during the holiday rush.

Another client's experience with a sales promotion illustrates the point beautifully. This man had a 20 year old retail business and he was ready to retire. He couldn't find a buyer for the business but he did sell the building, and he arranged to continue his business for eight months after the building was sold. In other words, we were able to plan an eight month "going out of business" sale!

It was unforgettable! For eight months customers stood in long lines to buy merchandise, while supplier trucks stood in line by the back door to deliver more. My client made so much money in those eight months that it really didn't matter whether he sold the business or not. As he sat in front of me exhausted and happy, he said, "Hal, if I were to go into business again, I think I'd have more sales."

"Going out of business" is the strongest reason for a sale but I think this illustrates my point. It's not so much the actual price. It's the reason you have for reducing the price that is most appealing for the customer. If the discounter's everyday prices are lower, there better be some perceived differences between what Bob and Dolores offer and what the discounters offer or they are in big trouble.

Bob and Dolores heard this and cried out in unison, "Okay, we're ready to go out of business and become millionaires. When do we start?"

"All in good time, all in good time," I replied. "Let's start by getting a handle on the problem. Have you spent much time at your competitor's stores?"

Bob replied, "To be honest, I've been in them a few times, but I haven't been at either one for at least a year."

"Me either," said Dolores.

I suggested they visit both competitors and look at their operations from a pricing point of view. I did the same. What we discovered was very interesting. It turned out that the discount book store actually was only "deep discounting" the best sellers. The other "deep discounts" were actually publisher's closeouts, usually books that the publishers could not sell at regular price so they discounted heavily to get rid of them. The discount book store probably had full margins on these closeouts. The rest of the books had only a 10% discount.

It was also obvious that the discount store had untrained help and were set up with national promotions. It was likely they would find it hard to respond to a local promotion.

The office supply discounter had selected only the most popular office supplies; they did not carry any other specialty supplies. Those were displayed in one aisle between groceries and television sets.

I told Bob and Dolores to try to establish a couple of tables for "bruised" books and those reduced for other reasons. They would become a permanent part of the store. I also suggested that some office supplies be discounted and displayed along with the books. They also bought more publisher's closeouts and changed the tables frequently. The combination of books on the closeout table created an interesting adventure for any book lover.

I also warned them to alert their staff to the purpose of these tables. I once told an owner of a similar kind of store to set up a "reduced" table only to find that three months later the store manager had taken it down. Her reason? Not many items on it were selling.

The purpose of a "reduced price table" is to give people a good reason to come into the store, not to sell a lot of reduced merchandise. Even people who did not intend to buy a book are enticed by the "reduced" sign. Over time, Bob and Dolores did sell a lot from the tables. They increased traffic in their store by creating a continuing impression that there were always bargains to be found.

"Shall we put best sellers on sale everyday?" asked Dolores. "We don't sell many since the discount store started up."

"That is a good question. I'm not sure about that one," I said. "You might test it. I think anytime you have 'reason' to reduce the price, I sure would. 'Bruised and reduced' is a good reason. But we need to come up with lots of other reasons."

We also talked before about setting up monthly promotions. I thought deep discounts on the best sellers and the popular office supplies should be included in these promotions. When you promote price, don't hold back. Shave that extra nickel or even penny. It makes such a difference.

> **$5.95 is a lot less than $6.00**

Customer perception is often more emotional than logical. Another retail client had a competitor on the next block. One day a customer came in and said she had bought an item from a competitor, but it had a defect. She tried to exchange it but the competitor was out of stock. My client had it in stock and sold it to her. The customer commented, "Oh, you're really not that much more expensive than they are." That perception shocked my client and she investigated. She found that she sold the item for the same price but that her competitor had a pricing policy of charging $5.95 for a $6.00 item. My client changed a lot of tags that night!

(By themselves, these pricing decisions were not crucial, but in combination with other decisions, they helped the Rafertys turn the tide and reestablish the book and office supply profit centers they had once enjoyed.)

Your price must allow you to make a profit

Most of the time Mike and Jim reflect the happy mood one might associate with making toys and games for kids. They seem like Santa's helpers. Not today. They look like accountants in tax season, surrounded by books and papers. It is catalogue review time with Mr. Retailer, their largest customer.

Mike and Jim could increase their prices anytime, but as a practical matter, the upcoming catalogue review will determine what their games will be selling for by mail order and in Mr. Retailer's stores during the next year. Since Mr. Retailer is their largest customer and accounts for half of sales, these pricing decisions go a long way toward determining the quality of their next year.

As I've often said, one of the nice things about working with small businesses is that no decision is that big. So if we make a mistake we can correct it and keep moving. This is true for almost all of my clients, except for Mike and Jim.

"It's not my favorite time of the year," said Mike. "If we blow this one, I'm going to apply to be an announcer with the Cubs."

"We've got to get this business expanded so that Mr. Retailer is not such a factor or we will all have ulcers," said Jim.

"Let's look at the problem at hand," I said. "If you've got your proposal prepared let's review it point by point. How do your prices look at the retail level next year?"

"Let's use our bubble gum baseball game as the example and the rest will follow," said Mike. "This year it is selling for $7.00 at retail and it's doing quite well. It might maintain sales at $8.00 and that may be the best way to go when we consider the whole picture."

Jim spoke, "We are getting cost increase pressure from suppliers and we are going to have to bump wages up soon. It looks like at least a 5% to 10% cost increase next year. As you know, profits are decent but nothing to get excited about. Mr. Retailer is screaming that the margins on our line are not good enough. I don't know if that is true or if they are just warming up for negotiations."

"Is Mr. Retailer going to drop anything from your line? How much discount does Mr. Retailer get?," I asked.

"Our sales have been holding and increasing on some games," said Jim. "The current discount schedule is 50% - 20% - 5% - 5%."

"Run that by again very slowly," I said.

"Okay," said Jim. "50% is the discount to the retailer. That means the retailer buys the $7 game for $3.50. 20% is the distributor's discount. That means the distributor buys the game for $2.80. The 5% discounts are for quantity purchases."

That means that Mr. Retailer with their large volume is paying Mike and Jim about $2.50 for the game. If the retail price is raised $1.00 you would get about $.35 more or $2.85 for the game. That sounds like it would cover your increased costs and increase Mr. Retailer's profits as well. I asked them if they were pretty confident that the price increase would not have an adverse impact on sales.

"It's been three years since we have increased the price, and the game continues to be very popular," Jim replied. "It seems to be well within the price range of other board games. We haven't mentioned it to Mr. Retailer yet, but we have talked to our other sales reps and they don't see a problem. They believe many game prices will be going up this year. What do you think, Mike?"

"Let's go for it," said Mike.

"What is your alternative if Mr. Retailer won't go along with the price increase?" I asked.

"That will be a problem," Jim responded. "That would wipe out our profits for next year. We're really caught up in a cost-price squeeze. We would have to reduce our costs somehow. We might acquire our own printing press and do the printing ourselves. We might have to have the game produced overseas. So much for the balance of payments. If Mr. Retailer really insists on holding the price, we will have to scramble to make any money next year."

"You mentioned that Mr. Retailer was 'screaming about the margins' on your line. What does that mean? Are they looking for additional discounts?"

"I don't know," said Jim. "That is a real worry because we are the small guys in the industry. Most of our competitors who make games are 100 or 200 times larger than we are. Who knows what kind of special discounts they are offering Mr. Retailer. We have been pushing for more store promotions of our products. I think we would be willing to give an advertising allowance for more promotions if push came to shove."

"Our relationship with Mr. Retailer has always been very good," said Mike. "I think we are a profitable line for them and the price increase will make us more profitable. I think we should press for more promotions and resist any advertising allowance."

"You sound very well prepared to me. Good luck. Go you Tigers."

"All in a day's work," said Jim.

(Mike and Jim prevailed for another year. The price increase was accepted but they did give an advertising allowance. Sales continued to be strong in the next year. This episode illustrates that pricing decisions are often made in stages. Mike and Jim had done their homework and decided what they would offer Mr. Retailer. The final pricing decisions were made in negotiations with Mr. Retailer.)

Now, let's shift gears. A "crucial" decision for most business owners is how to get more customers. Most small businesses quickly decide that TV is not in their budget. Let's explore some affordable ways to attract more customers, including the secret weapon of small business: "word of mouth".

Many small business owners think marketing is the fun part. There is a lot of room for imagination. Let's see if we can help our friends get more customers.

CHAPTER SEVEN

Deciding on Selling Methods: How Can I Sell More Without Spending More?

The secrets of selling

The biggest question in the minds of most start-up business owners is how they are going to sell their goods or services. A common attitude is that knowing how to sell requires having some secret knowledge. I'm often asked for the secret.

Actually, I think there are several "secrets" to selling. I've already talked about some of the important ones. If there is something wrong with your commitment, the quality of your goods or services, your perception of your customer, your location, or your pricing, don't expect some fancy selling tips to suddenly make your business successful. It won't happen.

Now I'm going to talk about one of the most important principles of selling. This "secret", simply stated, is that you sell to "warm" and not to "cold". An important part of the selling process is finding ways to change "cold" into "warm."

"You may not find out how warm the
prospect is until you try to close the sale."

"Warm" and "cold" will vary depending on the circumstances. For example, a close friend or relative who knows and likes what you do would probably be considered "hot," if he or she is in a position to help you. Someone you've been introduced to, or a person who has heard of you, could be considered warm. For instance, large companies spend millions of dollars to create brand name recognition, which is just another way of saying "warm."

How your product or service is used or how much it is needed will have a direct impact on how much "warm" you must create. For example, if you repair refrigerators, having an ad in the yellow pages may create enough warmth. I once used this example in a group discussion and someone said, "I know a very reliable person who repairs appliances." This confused my example because if any of us had a refrigerator breakdown in the next couple of months, I'm sure we would have called "old reliable." He would have been "warmer" than the yellow pages list. But after some time passed, we would probably forget the name and need to rely on the yellow pages again.

How big is your network?

Asking your first potential customer to buy whatever it is you have to sell is probably the single most difficult task involved in starting a business. The fear of rejection is enormous. I've seen new small business owners spend days straightening up their desks and even washing the office walls to avoid this rejection.

Therefore, Susan is acting pretty normal. She has

identified some questions she "must study" before she can begin to market. She is acting as though marketing will be like diving off a cliff into a sea of rejection.

"Okay, okay," said Susan, "I'm convinced that I have to get involved in selling my services. I suppose you want me to start cold calling the larger companies."

The words "cold calling" provided a big clue to Susan's attitude. To someone who is inexperienced in marketing, selling means cold calling. It represents the ultimate opportunity for rejection. In truth, "cold calling" is just one tool in the marketing tool box. Futhermore, unless it is used in a very controlled way, it is often a very ineffective technique. Cold calling may have a place in Susan's marketing program, but not immediately.

If sales are made more successfully to "warm" prospects, the major marketing question is, "What makes a prospect warm?" In Susan's case, the most obvious "warm" prospects are those who already know her and her work.

I advised Susan to make a list of all the people that she knew in the employee benefits field. I told her to call them up and tell them what she was doing. Susan did what I advised and within two months she was busy meeting with "warm" prospects about potential business.

When asked how long it will take to get a business going, I usually reply, "How big is your network?" In Susan's case, she had created a large warm network through her activities in her former job and with industry associations. She was known by many people who liked and respected her. It was not surprising that these old friends helped her get business leads. In fact, this is what one could have expected to happen.

What is networking?

The most important selling method for most small business owners is "networking." Networking is the best method of creating "word of mouth" publicity, and word of mouth selling is the secret weapon of the small business.

What is networking? I used to think it was going to a cocktail party and nervously shifting from one foot to another while trying to decide which conversation to break into. I finally discovered that the best way for me to "work" cocktail parties was to stand by the food. It's hard on the waistline, but it does ensure that you'll meet everyone at the party.

Networking is broader than a party. It's the process of meeting and getting to know people and, through them, meeting and getting to know other people. Keeping in touch with people in your network can be very productive. A few years ago it was actually a trendy thing for people to do. While giving a talk to a small group, I remarked that it was important for a business to network. I was surprised when several members of the audience told me that networking was "old stuff." They had done it and were tired of it. I was shocked until I discovered that these people were not business owners and didn't have a particular reason for networking.

In ancient times (prior to 1980), business networks were also known as "old boy" networks. These were relatively closed, comfortable groups of men who exchanged business opportunities, often in informal settings such as private clubs or on golf courses. The existence of the "old boy" networks, which by their nature excluded newly emerging women entrepreneurs, moved women to create networks of their own.

Women have brought business networking to a new level. They have gone far beyond the "old boy" networks, and this has been responsible for phenomenal business growth. Such success is probably a result of the tendency most women have to be more social than men are. When they apply these social skills in business situations, good things happen. But something else is also happening. It might be called "caring" networking, or "active listening" to determine other people's needs. This attitude makes women's networking especially effective.

It's easy to see how powerful a "caring" network can be. By helping others meet their needs, friendships and strong business alliances develop very quickly. It's a wonderful way to build a business.

However, one cautionary note: Business owners should define the kind of network they need. Networks can be used to find new customers, new suppliers, or even new employees. If you're looking for new customers what would your network look like? For some businesses it's enough to go out and make friends. For example, if you are building a general dentistry practice, you might as well attend any social function that appeals to you, because anyone can be your customer. But like Susan, many businesses must attract large corporate customers, so broad-based, hit and miss networking won't help much. She needs to do more than make a lot of friends.

Some years ago a woman who had started a business the previous year came to me for advice. When I asked her how big a network she had, I got the surprise of my life. She was an active member of about a dozen women's organizations. Everybody knew her. But from a business standpoint it didn't help. Few people knew what she actually did.

A network can be a great source of referrals. Word of mouth referrals mean that the potential customer is already warm. They will be inclined to buy from you because you are a known quantity. In order for your network to work for you, your network must know what you do. Just as important, your network must be aware that you are still alive.

A network doesn't necessarily have to be very large. I've seen some pretty successful businesses that were built on small networks. I remember the training company that had been in business for 15 years and had no consistent marketing program. Now and then this client would come to see me without any active business or even active prospects for business. Each time I would help him with some marketing ideas, but before he could implement them, he would suddenly get very busy again. When this pattern repeated itself a number of times over a couple of years, I suggested we try to figure out just what was happening.

It turned out that he had about 75 close friends and contacts, and whenever he didn't have any work he called them up. Magically, within a month or so, new customers would appear. All he had been doing was activating his network.

Whenever a business is in a slump and needs some immediate sales, I will often prescribe "Rolodex" marketing. Having an owner call his or her warm network is the fastest way to get a business going again.

A business without a warm network is very vulnerable. Another training company had been working successfully with just a handful of clients over a period of ten or twelve years. Whenever the business lost a client, there seemed to be another waiting in the wings. However, one day a client was lost and there wasn't another just waiting to appear. Ironically, at the same time, other clients cut back on the services they were purchasing and the business was suddenly in trouble. Unfortunately, there was no warm network, mainly because the business had always done so well over the years, and so they hadn't seemed to need one. A very difficult period followed in which a network was developed.

Keeping in touch

From my work with direct mail, I've developed a theory that the average person's active memory is a little over two months. Let's say you are a plumber. You meet Mr. and Mrs. Average at a party. During the next two months, if anyone asks this couple if they know a plumber, chances are they will mention you. But if they are asked the same question six months later, the Averages probably won't think of you. You are no longer in their active memory. They would likely remember you if your name came up, but they wouldn't think of you on their own.

If you are relying on a network for business referrals, you had better call those in the network every couple of months. If you have a large network, I strongly advocate sending a mailing every two or three months.

When I started my business consultation practice, I created about 500 contacts in a few months. I didn't have time to stay in touch either by phone or by face-to-face contact so I began to publish a newsletter every two months. I've continued to do this as my network has grown, and prospective clients are constantly referred to me by my network.

The newsletter is a good tool for changing cold prospects to warm over a period of time. Susan's business is a good case in point. Obviously, it would be a good idea for Susan to send a newsletter or some kind of mailing to her business friends every couple of months. In addition, Susan might want to target a number of companies who don't—but should—know about her. They should be added to the mailing list for her newsletter. Over a period of time, as these companies become familiar with Susan, they will become warm potential customers for her services.

This technique can be used for all potential customers, no matter how small the number. One of my professional-practice clients hasn't wanted to commit to a newsletter. However, there is one prospect so potentially valuable that he decided to produce a "newsletter for one." (I've heard of worse ideas. It will probably work.)

Most small business owners are willing to do marketing mailings. They certainly rank it high above cold calling. They won't be rejected, even though it might be more effective to call prospective customers and be rejected sometimes.

A painting contractor who specializes in large commercial jobs decided to do a series of mailings which offered helpful painting tips. This particular client was especially timid about selling his services to "strangers."

His "painting tips" campaign was well received. Each tip was interesting and he sent them to commercial buildings which his research identified as his best prospective customers. Sending out these tips every couple of months for a year would make him well known to painting purchasers in the area and give him an opportunity to bid on many jobs. Then he asked, "What if I send the mailing to the wrong person?

What if the purchaser never sees it? I'll be wasting my stamps."

I agreed that there was a problem and suggested that he call each company to get the name of the buyer of painting services. He started a telephone campaign to get this information. During the first week, one person asked him why he wanted the information. When he answered, the person said the company had a painting project and asked him if he wanted to bid on it. This resulted in his landing a huge painting job. As you can imagine, his attitude toward calling prospective buyers changed a lot. He became an avid caller and his business prospered greatly. A large part of marketing is momentum.

Cold marketing — Ten Plus Ten

The combination of sending a letter to a prospect and following it with a telephone call is much, much more effective than just writing a letter. In many situations, this combination will identify <u>ten times</u> more prospects than a mailing alone.

Suppose you send a mailing out to a thousand prospects and get 20 responses. Depending on the situation this could be considered highly successful. If you followed up on those 1,000 prospects by telephone, you could expect 200 responses. What a difference!

The reason for this difference is not super salesmanship on the phone. The natural tendency for the prospective purchaser to procrastinate on the buying decision is the biggest reason for this increased success. Most of the time, people don't react immediately to an offer even if they have a strong interest in it. The phone call is necessary to activate that interest.

Knowing this proves useful in many types of selling situations. One of my favorite techniques is called "ten plus ten." It's really "ten plus ten plus ten." The first week's work is to identify 10 specific prospects by name. The second week's job is to send 10 letters, and during the third week the task is to make 10 follow-up phone calls.

When you identify ten new prospects each week, this becomes a consistent marketing program which is often effective even in "cold" situations. I suggest it for many types of businesses, like Susan's, where the prospects are limited and identifiable and the sale is a potentially large one. As it's turning out, Susan's warm network is so large she may never have to use cold calling techniques to get new prospects.

Selling to your existing customers

Some years ago I worked with a dentist who had moved his office just a few blocks and had seen his busy practice fall off drastically. It was quite a shock—and a mystery. The new location looked all right. A fine job had been done in announcing the move to all of his patients.

After a lot of investigation, we decided that the only thing different, in addition to the location, was that a part-time receptionist had decided not to make the move. She would have had to take an extra bus to get to the new office and she wasn't willing to do it. That receptionist had been responsible for rebooking old patients and for making reminder calls the day before an appointment.

Luckily, the dentist was able to pay for her cab rides and rehire this receptionist. Her special "gift of gab" made her effective at befriending the patients and convincing them to keep their appointments. Business boomed again. This incident has always made me especially impressed by the power of <u>anyone</u> who has direct contact with customers.

Selling the big score—
12 around the corner

Susan was excited. On her first sales call to a big company, the executive she had talked to was very positive about her services. She got about the same reaction at the second big company.

Susan was on "Cloud Nine;" her feet didn't touch the ground. She had been so worried about selling her services, and such good responses from the first two potential clients was more than she had hoped for. Now she knew her business would be very successful. I asked her how the situation was left with each of these prospects.

"In both cases, they asked me to call them next month and we would get going then." said Susan. "There is no point in doing much more marketing. Either of these companies could keep me busy for a long time."

It was true. Either of these clients could give Susan enough consulting work to keep her busy virtually around the clock. Susan is in what I call "a big score" business. That simply means that each "sale" could be worth a lot of money. In Susan's case, $10,000-$20,000 or more.

There are certain characteristics that surround a "big

score" sale, and they have an impact on the strategy one needs to use in making the sale. For example, there is usually difficulty in identifying and getting to the decision makers. In fact, the decision process may be hard to identify. Often it's hard to tell precisely where you stand.

In order to successfully sell the big score, I think you have to adopt the attitude that you need "12 around the corner." "Around the corner" means the sale could be consummated tomorrow and it would not be surprising. I've seen many, many examples where business failed to materialize until there were about a dozen of these possibilities, all of which, or none of which, could happen tomorrow. This means you must keep hustling after business even when the big scores appear to be almost certain. In other words, it's not a deal until it's a "done deal."

I strongly advised Susan to keep on calling her friends and lining up warm prospects. She agreed, a smart move because a month later she called the company to whom she had made her first sales call. The conversation went something like this:

Susan: "Larry, this is Susan."

Larry: "Susan who?"

Susan: "Susan Andrews, Jerry's friend, the consultant."

Larry: "Oh Susan, thanks for calling. We've really been busy lately. Haven't had a chance—tell you what, give me a call next month."

Obviously, Larry is just one of Susan's "12 around the corner" prospects.

Evaluating your advertising

Most business owners try to sell their goods or services in a wide variety of ways. However it is often difficult to determine which selling methods are working and which are not.

Advertising can be very expensive. If it works, it can be very <u>inexpensive</u>. You must discover what techniques work for you. Since starting out, Cindy's basic "prospecting" expense has been the telephone book. Most of her customers have found out about her moving services simply by looking in the yellow pages.

Cindy advertises in a large number of phone books in virtually every wealthy suburb in her area. This advertising expense has been increased for two reasons. The first is that there are now competing yellow page phone books. Any business owner who relies on these advertising pages for business is almost forced to be in all of them to insure that the market is being reached. The other reason is a result of a trick used by today's yellow page companies to expand business. Nowadays, big discounts are being offered to lure competitors into larger ads, causing all the competing companies to spend a lot more to compete with each other in the yellow pages.

A look at Cindy's expense statement made us wonder if the purpose of her business might not be to make the phone book publishers rich. She became increasingly unhappy with these figures, and she began to carefully track the source of each new customer. This enabled her to discontinue some advertising. Cindy also decided to have her yellow page ads produced by a professional, enabling her to run smaller ads that drew more response because of their superior design. Ultimately, she reduced her total expense.

Spending more money is not a guarantee of more sales. There are many other things involved in increasing sales. For example, I had a hand in a 30% rise in Cindy's business with one simple idea. Cindy often moves people in or out of luxury apartment buildings. I suggested that Cindy post an attractive advertising sign on the bulletin boards in all these buildings. It was a bit of a hassle to keep the signs up and looking good, but they paid big dividends for a very small investment. Over time, the tenants in several large buildings came to consider Cindy as the "mover of choice."

So, what is the best advertising for Cindy, yellow pages or bulletin boards? The answer, of course, is that both are best, even though the yellow pages are more expensive than we'd like them to be. There are some simple principles behind these ideas, but the basic one is: You sell to warm, not cold, whenever you can.

Simply put, warm is a satisfied customer. Warm is friends and relatives. Warm includes someone who sees your sign every day for a year. You become a "brand name." This is why the bulletin board sign works so well for Cindy. Warm would also be someone who needs your services and looks you up in the yellow pages. In Cindy's case, defining these "warm situations" was a prelude to the sales process.

The sales process

When examining the sales process it pays to look at all the details right down to the words being spoken. I once worked with a landscaping company whose staff made sales over the phone using newspaper leads. We didn't think they were making as many sales as they should be, so I asked them to tape a few of the phone conversations for me.

I played the tape while I was doing some paper work one evening. I listened with pride as my client projected a positive image and asked all the right questions. "There's a sale!" I thought. There was a pause in the conversation. "Close, close, close," I said to myself. Then I heard my client's voice say, "If you give me your address I'll be happy to send you some literature." I jumped out of my chair, raced to the phone, called my client and told him to start <u>asking</u> for the sale. Sales doubled that night!

For small business owners, "closing" the sale is the most common problem area in the sales process. Like the landscaper, they may not try to close at all. After all, if you don't close, you can't be rejected.

"I don't mind being rejected," said Cindy, "but I'd sure like to improve my sales."

For every moment you talk you move away from the sale; For every moment you listen you move toward the sale

I think the most important part of the sales process is listening. Ask your leading question or questions and then listen. If you ask the right questions and really listen you should find out what your prospect needs. You can then identify whether what you have to sell will satisfy those needs. If it can, point that out and ask for the sale.

This is a process you could call "active listening." You are trying to make sure that you and your prospect are talking about the same things. Be sure and ask questions any time you don't understand what's being said.

Listening is a very effective sales tool. When you are really listening, your prospective customers will assume that you understand their circumstances. Therefore, your recommendation will have more credibility. Hence my rule of thumb: For every minute you talk you move away from the sale, and for every minute you listen you move toward the sale. In other words, the more you know about the client and the job prior to making your offer, the more likely it is that you will actually close the sale. Listening is a lot more effective than "beating your chest" about how good you are.

"I do love to talk," said Cindy. "I wonder how many sales I've talked myself out of. I also think I make too many assumptions and don't ask enough questions. I'm going to start asking more questions. But what about the timing? When do I close the sale?"

When to close the sale

I think you should attempt to close the sale any time all the facts, including the price, have been stated. The words you say to close the sale should not be accidental. Many of my clients will have a stock phrase that they use every time they start to close. One of the favorite phrases is: "Now is a busy time of the year," followed by a question such as, "What do you think?", or "When do you want to get started?", or "I have an opening on the 15th." The sales person must then shut his or her mouth and wait for the prospect to respond.

When you close, you don't necessarily expect a "yes." More often than not you will get an objection. Objections can be valid questions that need to be answered or emotional reasons not to make a decision, or a "kind" way to say "no." Hardly anybody ever says just plain "no" to anything.

Each objection should be answered and once it is, the closing procedure should begin again. This process can repeat itself over and over again in complex sales situations. The closing process is there to help a potential buyer come to a decision. A professional sales person will have worked out answers to almost every objection, and will follow this process to get either a "yes" or a "no."

A sales call that doesn't end in either a "yes" or a "no" creates a spinning wheel. Spinning wheels must be followed. This is time consuming, thankless work which often ends in failure.

How to stop spinning wheels

Anytime you have had a sales meeting and you have not made an offer that can be accepted, you have wasted your time and you may have created a "spinning wheel." Even if you have not determined what it is you would sell to the prospect, you should make a specific offer for another meeting if you want to do business with this person.

"Spinning wheels" create false hope and can cause you to feel "secure" in your murky perceptions of a sure sale. This often ends in disaster.

A spinning wheel is worse than being rejected because of the continuing emotional and mental effort which goes into the follow-up. One of my clients had made a career out of creating spinning wheels. He saw the light and developed a new policy. He identified his problem as fear of rejection. He then determined that he would have a goal of being rejected at least once a day. This idea made him a lot more effective.

The best way to stop spinning wheels is to never let them get started. Sometimes this can't be done. As previously discussed, the "big scores" are particularly hard to pin down. Therefore, it is necessary that the customer have a reason to "do it now."

In the sales process it is particularly important to listen for "when's." If you can identify that your prospect needs something by a specific date, you can stop the spinning wheel. The fact that a sale price is in effect for only a limited time is often more important than the amount of the discount.

One of the most distraught clients I've ever worked with had exceeded my "12 around the corner" rule of thumb.

He had 17 spinning wheels, each worth about $10,000. This situation was the product of an amateur sales person who didn't know how to close a sale. My client was climbing the walls trying to follow up on these 17 potential customers.

We devised a short term promotion program designed to get the prospects either in or out. We reasoned that we would be ahead if they all said no. In fact 15 did say no, but two agreed. It was a good day.

(Stronger closing techniques resulted in more sales for Cindy, but even more important there were fewer spinning wheels. With the time and emotional burden of spinning wheels reduced, Cindy's entire attitude toward the business improved.)

Publicity is the most powerful marketing tool

Alex is full of sales ideas; he's tried them all—special ads, coupons, door hangers. He's always got a promotional gimmick going. Somehow, they all work, but none of them really works, because business stays about the same.

Alex is always asking me to come up with more gimmicks. I'm continually asking him to improve his food. What's the use of attracting more people into the restaurant if the food isn't good enough to bring them back?

Alex frequently talks about the early days, back when the restaurant first opened. There was a big write-up in the local newspaper and at first the business boomed. What Alex described is the normal life-cycle for a restaurant. When a restaurant opens it attracts its natural following, usually those people who live or work close by and need a place to eat.

Then a write-up in the local paper brings hordes of people wanting to "try it out." Unfortunately, the average restaurant is unable to maintain service or quality in the face of these crowds, so the crowds don't come back. Regrettably, the natural following is also discouraged by the crowds so they stop coming too.

Publicity is a very powerful tool. It works. It can work too well if you're not ready to take advantage of it.

Publicity is based on news. What is new about Alex's place? The idea of catering to the "after- theatre-crowd" is new. It was time for the creative juices to start flowing. Alex talked to the theater management and he got a schedule of movies for the month ahead. We picked out a coming blockbuster that had a gangster theme.

Alex decorated the restaurant in a 30's motif and dressed waitresses like molls with black stockings and garters. We called all the local newspapers. One editor liked the idea and gave us a half-page spread. (We suspected that they chose to take pictures because one of the waitresses had "Betty Grable" legs.) It worked. The after-theater-dinner-crowd has been equal to the breakfast crowd ever since the article came out.

Planning — the key to promotions

I didn't think there was much I could teach Bob and Dolores about selling their merchandise. They had been doing that very successfully for years. But as I worked with them, I noticed that they were always scrambling to get ads prepared and in the paper. There is no question that Bob and

Dolores had a plan to run the business. They controlled purchasing and staffing, but advertising and promotion came more as an afterthought.

I had Bob and Dolores lay out a month by month promotional scheme. Many months posed no problem. Christmas, Easter, Thanksgiving and "back-to-school" promotions fell right into place. But this approach pointed out how empty the summer months were, the worst months for Bob and Dolores. Because there were no promotions planned, slow business during these months had become a self-fulfilling prophecy.

Since there were no exciting things going on in the summer, we needed to create some excitement. Creating excitement is a part of selling that is especially fun. It's a matter of brainstorming to come up with some ideas that your customers will think are fun too.

Creating special sale days in cooperation with other businesses in your area is a common and often successful way of turning slow times into effective promotional periods. Bob and Dolores became very interested in this approach. They were instrumental in creating a festival weekend in July. The street was closed and half the town was in front of their store eating hot dogs and breaking balloons. (Bob and Dolores sold the balloons.)

Sometimes the value of these promotions comes more from accidental publicity than from direct sales at the time. For example, when a bike shop sponsored the "Bike Ride in Hawaii Weekend" during the coldest days of winter, both the newspapers and television stations picked it up. It became one of the big "happenings" of the week. It was a family event with people riding stationary bikes in the store while watching a video tape of the Hawaiian bike ride.

Even more interesting was the reaction to the Marble Championship which a toy store sponsored for local kids one July. The kids didn't respond because they are not into marbles these days. The contest all but died. But all the adults, including those in the media, thought it was such a great idea that it received big publicity in a normally dead time of the year.

Trade shows mean opportunity

Sometimes I think that the greatest marketing service that I can provide to my clients is to check to see if they have given their prospective customers a reason to "buy now." Without a reason to do it now, lot of merchandise and services would never be sold.

One could argue that the most important ingredient in making the economy run is the trade show. The trade show gives people a reason to do it now. New product development and fresh marketing literature are invariably tied to trade shows. Many businesses would never progress without them.

Until now, Mike and Jim have defined selling as standing in back of their table for three days at the National Game Show. Every year by the last day of the show, it was clear that Mike and Jim would become multimillionaires. Everyone loved their products.

But during the next week, reality always asserted itself again. Mike and Jim's line was not broad enough to be attractive to most distributors. They are too small, and promises are not always kept. On the other hand, the National Game Show is where "Mr. Retailer" first found Mike and Jim, so hope springs eternal. Perhaps another "Mr. Retailer" will surface.

I prefer "planning" to "hope," so I started to ask some questions. What were Mike and Jim trying to accomplish at the show? Were they planning to write orders? Were they trying to make contact with retailers and distributors? How were they going to follow-up with those who showed interest? How did they plan to attract people at the show?

Mike and Jim did have a good plan for attracting a crowd at the Game Show. They played games and it worked. But they really had no answer to the rest of my questions. It wasn't clear what they wanted to accomplish. There might be some follow-up phone calls to hot prospects, but otherwise they were waiting for lightning to strike. After all, it had already struck once. Perhaps it would strike again.

The trade show was not one at which on the spot orders were routinely written. But many contacts were made that could be followed up. Mike and Jim decided that they really wanted to identify large retail stores. We devised a prize drawing that was attractive to retailers and allowed us to get some specific information about them. We came out of the show with a hot list that was easy to follow up on. Lightning didn't strike again, but enough post-show sales were made to pay for the cost of the show many times over.

Direct mail — marketing by the numbers

The idea of selling by mail has really intrigued Mike and Jim. This does appear to be the most logical method for getting their advanced baseball game into game players' hands.

There are some advantages to direct mail over other forms of marketing. Direct mail is very repeatable and predictable. Once you find something that works, you can repeat it over and over again. If something doesn't work you know that too. There are no maybe's. The check is either in the mail or it isn't and if it isn't, another approach must be tried. Those who are experienced in other types of business usually encounter a major problem when they do direct mail because of the level of detailed record keeping that is required. I liken it to putting together a jigsaw puzzle. The question is always: What response do we get when we send a particular letter to a particular group?

Mike and Jim are testing many variables and trying to get answers about what is most effective. For example, they run ads in some carefully selected magazines asking people to send in coupons for more information. They are also sending their literature directly to people on selected lists such as subscribers to baseball magazines.

One way to learn the mail order business is to pay close attention to what comes into your mail box on a regular basis. Whether or not it strikes your fancy, you can bet that if a large mailing is repeated, it worked very well the first time. The large mailers have obviously tested their pieces very thoroughly. They've taken the guess work out of it.

Mike and Jim are getting some mail order sales.

However I don't know if they have the commitment yet to this side of the business and the attention to detail that it requires.

The best marketing method: satisfied customers

Meanwhile, the only marketing effort that has really been important to Mike and Jim has been keeping Mr. Retailer happy. Someday, someone will write a book about the technique of keeping one large customer happy over a period of years. It will be a best seller and Mike and Jim might write it. But my best efforts will still be on expanding the customer base. One big customer is too risky for any business.

That sounds like negative thinking, but it's thinking that must be heeded. There is, however, an extremely positive side to Mike and Jim's situation. They sell to warm. They sell to a satisfied customer and that's as warm as you can get.

This is the ultimate point of this chapter. In order to be successful at selling, you need to sell to warm. The questions you must ask yourself are "What is warm?", and "How can I turn cold to warm?" It's the real secret to selling.

CHAPTER EIGHT

The Financial Decision I—Working Capital: Does It Take Money to Lose Money?

Lack of money causes panic

This chapter, and the following one, are written especially for those of you whose eyes glaze over when finances are mentioned. You know who you are. You are the business owners who leave the financial statements from your accountant in unopened envelopes. Down deep you probably believe that if you took those statements from their envelopes and actually studied them, you would understand the financial side of your business. Wrong! Chances are good it would not help much. And that is not because you are dumb about finances.

You will not understand your business by looking at your financial statements because that's not what they're for. Financial statements for small businesses are prepared primarily for income tax purposes, not to give you information with which you can make decisions about your business. (I'll discuss this idea in greater detail in the next chapter which is devoted to helping you determine how much profit you are making.)

*"You try a lot of ways to raise
working capital."*

132

For now, let's focus on working capital decisions. Working capital is just another way of saying "money." Lack of money is the cause of many "emotional" decisions in small businesses. After all, money is needed to pay creditors, the rent, the payroll—and <u>yourself</u>. When you are short of money for any of these purposes, your life as an owner can be a painful mess. At such times, you will find yourself scrambling about trying to save your credit and maintain your employees and yourself by finding cash transfusions.

The lack of money has little to do with the success of a business. Some very successful businesses continually scramble after money. In fact, it is very dangerous to judge how a business is doing by the amount of cash it has available. When a business grows, often the first thing that happens is that the cash disappears because it goes into more inventory or larger accounts receivable.

Yet, when even a successful business runs out of money, an owner panics. The rent must be paid! The payroll must be covered! Money must be available to do these things. It is easy to see why an otherwise successful small business owner could make all kinds of disastrous decisions because: "I don't have enough money." It's the factor that makes working capital decisions <u>crucial</u>.

In other words, it's crucial for you to determine how much money you need in your business and how to get it or you may make all kinds of bad decisions because you don't think you have enough money.

Where did all my money go?

Jim and Mike are among my most successful clients. They have had a very profitable business for a long time. "We seem to have run out of money," said Jim, "Business is great. We picked up a lot of new sales, but we don't have any cash."

This is a familiar story to me—a successful, profitable, and growing business runs out of money. This was a discouraging turn of events for Mike and Jim—and just when things were going so well. What a problem. No money. They started talking about cutting back. "Perhaps we should delay the test mailings for our direct marketing project," suggested Mike.

My first task was to calm them down. In some ways they had become spoiled. Having one big customer like Mr. Retailer was stressful, but they hadn't had any money worries because this major customer paid them as soon as their invoices were received. Mr. Retailer would also give them orders in advance so they never had to build much of an inventory of finished goods.

It wasn't hard to figure out what was going on. Mike and Jim had picked up some new customers from a trade show. These new customers didn't pay as quickly as Mr. Retailer, so accounts receivable were higher. To put it very simply, if our customers owe us money, we don't have that money.

The new customer also wanted the merchandise right away and would not schedule orders in advance, so Mike and Jim had to have more inventory to meet their needs. If our money is tied up in inventory, we don't have that money either.

In addition, in order to handle the growing business,

Mike and Jim have bought a new computer system. This was a purchase that was long overdue. The new system is helping them streamline their operations and it will save them a lot of money. But again, if our money is tied up in equipment, we don't have that money.

Mike and Jim have become a classic example of a successful business short on money. They are experiencing all three of the most common reasons for running out of money—accounts receivable, inventory, and new equipment. There is nothing wrong with having your money tied up in these three ways. As long as the accounts receivables don't get too old, and the inventory and equipment are not excessive, you should expect to have money tied up in these items. But, that doesn't solve the basic problem of being out of money.

Money needs can be predicted

Small business owners develop their own methods of scrambling around for money. I'm constantly amazed at the resourcefulness that is put into this activity. My own father had a daily ritual he practiced for over 30 years. He raced from bank to bank with certified checks. It was his activity from about noon to 2 p.m. every day. He had one bank so well trained that if he had not shown up by 2 p.m., they would call his office to ask if he was coming.

Over this 30 year period, a rich family history was compiled—from speeding tickets to snow storms—while dad moved his money around. The point I want to make is that over the course of his career my father was probably a millionaire three times and broke three times and his daily scrambling for money never changed.

I've always wondered what would happen if the effort which is devoted to raising cash was instead focused on making more money. Perhaps we would be a nation of millionaires.

You need to be careful that the pressure of coming up with the cash doesn't cause a lot of other decisions which are detrimental to the business. Such a decision might be: "I haven't got enough money to advertise." Enough of these decisions can sink an otherwise healthy business.

One of the worst examples I've seen of a poor money decision was an owner who regularly camped on his best customer's doorstep to pick up a check which wasn't even due yet. He eventually alienated and lost his best customer with this procedure. There had to be a better way.

Actually, it is relatively easy to predict when you will need money. You can accurately predict when you will need to pay the rent, the payroll, and suppliers. Likewise, in many businesses you can fairly accurately identify when you will receive money.

Therefore, preplanning your money flow is usually a fruitful process and not nearly as complicated as it sounds. The point is that if you know when you are likely to run out of money, you should be able to take logical steps to keep it from being a problem. For example, in my own consulting business, I discovered that I pay out double the money in January that I do in August, and it is not related at all to the money coming in. Knowing this allows me to plan my commitments.

Many small business owners have a great reluctance to borrow money. Sometimes it's because they feel a loss of independence by having a lender looking over their shoulder. This attitude can unnecessarily slow the growth of the business when it directly relates to receivables, inventory, or equipment. The best solution is to get a loan to expand the money available to the business.

It is interesting to note that receivables, inventory, and equipment, along with land and buildings are the most common collateral for business loans. The solution in Mike and Jim's case was to obtain a loan in the form of a line of credit. This means that Mike and Jim can borrow money immediately when they need it and only have to pay interest for the period until they repay the money.

If you are serious about the growth of your business, it's important to establish a good relationship with a lending institution or else you won't grow—you'll run out of money.

Money problems in a marginal business

Up to now, we've been talking about running out of money in a successful business. As you would assume, running out of money in a less successful business is even more of a trauma and is a significant problem.

Alex spends more time with his cash flow than he does running the restaurant. At this stage, Alex's primary source of working capital is his accounts payable. Accounts payable is the money that you owe other people. In Alex's case these are the companies that sell him food and supplies. The reason it takes so much of his time is that they call all day long trying to get Alex to pay them. This has been going on every day for the last ten years.

As you can imagine, Alex is the "Grand Master" of the art of survival. Everything he has is in hock, yet he survives. I still can't tell you how.

Alex's money shortage stems from one fact. His business is not profitable. By this I mean that the expenses of running the business are greater than the money the business takes in. It wouldn't do much good to lend Alex a lot of money. If he didn't change anything, he would be right back in the same soup in a short time. The only long-term solution is to increase sales which would make this a profitable business. What Alex needs is good marketing decisions, not loans or investments.

Make sure you don't have a leak in your money system

There is one more hole to plug to make sure your money isn't escaping the business. One long-time client had the common problem: "I've run out of money," but, we couldn't spot the cause right away. It was a mystery.

We investigated accounts receivable, inventory, and equipment and found nothing unusual to explain where the money had disappeared. It also looked as if the business was still very profitable. Finally I asked him if he took a salary from the business. "Oh, no," he replied. "I don't take a salary. I just take money out when I need it."

There was a moment of silence and then he began to recall some events of the past couple of months. I heard him muttering "moved mother-in-law...paid taxes...car repairs...," etc. Much to my amazement, in a matter of minutes, he was able to recall about $40,000 that he had spent on personal matters in the last six weeks. The working capital mystery was solved.

It's your money, but I strongly advise you to identify a regular salary for yourself which will cover your personal expenses. This is especially important if you intend to borrow any money. It is too easy for it to slip away.

Obviously, this client had spent money without making decisions about his money supply. A disturbing effect was that his business began to look less profitable to him, even though the problem had nothing to do with the business.

Start-up money is usually "love" money

Susan beamed. It was clear that she thought she had discovered a gold mine. She had attended a workshop for start-up businesses which had talked about government loans.

"I've been thinking of borrowing at least $50,000." said Susan, "That would allow me to really get my business started right." I asked Susan what she would use the money for. Starting a consulting business does not necessarily require a lot of capital. There may be some office and marketing start-up costs, but the largest risk is the owner's personal financial commitment during the start-up period.

On the other hand, Susan could probably qualify for a loan because she has the "3 Cs" that a lender looks for—character, credit, and collateral. Even if Susan's business failed, Susan would probably be in a position to eventually repay any loan. She is a good risk.

It should be understood that banks and others who lend money do not wish to take risks. They are interested in timely repayment of loans with interest. Since starting a new business involves more unknowns than operating a continuing business, there is more risk involved. Because of this higher risk, it's hard to find lenders willing to loan money to start a business.

In addition to lenders, there are people called venture capitalists who will provide money to start a business in return for part ownership (or an equity share, as it's called) of the business. These venture capitalists are risk-takers, and they will demand substantial rewards for taking that risk.

Both the lenders and the venture capitalists will want to see that you have made a major investment before they will involve themselves. Even then, you will probably not be overwhelmed with people willing to advance you money. In fact, you will probably have to search for a lender or investor and you may never find one.

The major source of money to start a business could be called "love money." Love money is your personal savings or credit, or money coming from friends and relatives in the form of either loans or investments.

Susan is starting her business with savings from an employee benefit plan from her prior employer. This is a common source of capital for starting a business—company saving plans have multiplied over the last decade. Another common source is the increased value of homes. Many businesses are started with the proceeds from home equity loans.

If you are really short of capital, your best bet may be to find somebody who is trying to sell the type of business you'd like to start. Under many circumstances there may be an opportunity to buy a business without money. This might involve agreements to work for reduced wages to get ownership, or it could involve paying for the business out of future earnings.

Susan has enough money to get her business started and to survive for the first year even if she doesn't do any business. She could borrow some more money, but it isn't clear how that money would be used.

(Susan decided that she had enough capital for now. There were two factors that clinched the decision. First, it was evident that getting a loan for her business would be hard work. Her time would be better spent finding new clients. Secondly, a loan would have to be paid back with interest, so before she borrows money she should have a better use for it than she can identify right now.)

Money needs – survival to growth

Cindy has all sorts of uses for more money. Cindy has had to stretch and scramble ever since she started out. It took over a year to raise the money to buy her first truck and get her moving license.

Cindy's money problems vary from issues of day-to-day survival to long term growth. A few big moves can provide Cindy with a lot of money. She has to be careful how she spends it because large expenses, some of which are unexpected, are common in the moving business. She has to pay high insurance bills, and truck breakdowns can cost her thousands of dollars.

The problem of being able to keep her experienced

employees on the payroll during the slow winter months has caused Cindy many sleepless nights.

This problem may now be solved because of a contract she has with an appliance company to move refrigerators all year round. This should provide her with enough money during the winter to meet payroll.

The biggest money problem that Cindy has is growth. In order to grow she must invest in more trucks and that takes a lot of money. Even though the business is becoming profitable, she is not going to be able to buy more trucks from those profits. She must find additional sources of money.

Lenders vs. Investors

There are two common sources of new money for an existing business: loans and investments. Each has its advantages and its perils. If a business is "squared away" and profitable it should be able to borrow money. In fact, some financial experts will insist that a business always owe some money. In other words, long-term debt should be part of the capitalization or money structure of the company. Borrowing isn't all bad.

The problem with debt is that it must be repaid on time with interest, or the business may lose its credit standing. Paying off a lot of debt can reduce profits.
When you take on a lot of debt, you are betting that you can grow and increase your profits fast enough to pay the money back.

If your business is looked upon as too risky to qualify

for a loan, your alternative is to look for investor (or equity) money. An investor is buying part of your business. In other words, you have a partner. The advantage of an investor is that you are able to get money when you otherwise couldn't and there usually isn't any definite date by which it must be repaid. If things don't work out as planned you can always tell the investor that things will be better next year. You could be in big trouble if you tried to tell that to a bank with an overdue loan.

The biggest problem with having investors can be the investors themselves. People who have money to invest tend to believe they can also aid the business with their "management skills." While this may seem logical, I've never seen it work out.

I've worked with many growing, profitable companies that had "silent" partners who were the investors. This is a good arrangement. I've also worked with companies that took on <u>working</u> partners who were also investors. They were successful as well.

The situation that doesn't seem to work out is when the investor tries to become a part-time decision maker in the business. It doesn't work because the investor is making decisions based on his other business interests and not on the facts or needs of your particular business.

Business owners often come to me after they have received awful advice. When I ask them who advised them so badly, it is most typically a well-intentioned relative who has been very successful in business. It's obvious that the advice given was based on the facts of the relative's business and not on my client's specific case. I think this is the one factor that often makes investor advice so inept.

The business plan

Cindy's business is on the borderline with respect to the choice of pursuing a loan or an investor. She might be able to qualify for a loan and she probably could attract an investor. In either case, the first step is to have Cindy prepare a business plan.

I look at the business plan as a marketing campaign to raise money. The document itself is a marketing tool and the owner is the salesperson. It is essential that the owner thoroughly understand the plan, therefore the owner should at least write the first draft.

When the presentation is made, a lender or investor is going to be evaluating two things—the owner and the plan. Frankly, the most important evaluation is that made of the owner. If the lender or investor "buys" the owner, they'll probably buy the plan. Cindy is capable of making such an outstanding presentation of her business that I'm confident she'll eventually get the money she needs.

If confidence in the owner is lost, even the best plan will probably not save the day. A client once confided to me that his banker asked him if the profit shown was after the owner's salary was paid. My client didn't know and he should have. His presentation and hopes for a larger loan faded on the spot.

I think the way to start a business plan is to do a first draft of the executive summary. This is a page or two which describes the plan and how much money is needed. An owner can clarify his or her thoughts and focus on what is important. If you have drafted a good executive summary, the rest of the business plan may be nothing more than proving what the summary has asserted.

A business plan is a lot of work and pain. It will remind you of the term paper you did on Puerto Rico in the 8th grade. But for this term paper you will probably need some expert advice. Once you do a first draft, you should have a professional writer carve it up for you. (A free lance writer who specializes in business writing is a logical choice.)

You also need to get your accountant involved, but be sure you discuss your plan thoroughly before you have your accountant prepare the financial exhibits. Beware of self doubt.

The overly pessimistic business plan

My clients were going after a $250,000 loan and the business plan was over 100 pages. My clients and I were scheduled to meet Saturday to review the plan which was going to be presented to a bank the following week. The clients dropped the plan at my house on Friday so that I would have a chance to look at it before our meeting.

I didn't arrive home until 11 p. m. that Friday night. I noticed the plan and decided to thumb through it even though I was tired. I'd had a lot to do with the development of some key ideas in the business so the plan seemed to be making sense to me. Then I examined the financial statements. There was a monthly cash flow statement that showed the $250,000 entering the business. Each month a loss was projected. In fact, after 12 months of predicted losses the money was all gone. My reaction to this paper was simple. I decided I was too tired and went to bed.

The next morning I awoke and looked at this statement again and nothing had changed. I even asked my son, who knows nothing about finances, what he thought when he looked at it. "Well Dad," he said, "it looks as if this $250,000 comes in and then it's lose, lose, lose until they're out of money."

When my clients arrived I had a big grin on my face. "You are the first turkeys I've ever seen," I said, "who predicted their date of bankruptcy when they were trying to get a bank loan." They told me that their accountant had told them not to make the numbers too "optimistic."

Don't sell yourself short. When you are trying to put together your future, it is easy for self doubt to creep in. Your business plan needs to be as realistic as you can make it.

Doing what you say you will

Bob and Dolores have never done a formal business plan, but they have a lot of experience borrowing money. They were heavily in debt years ago, but as the business has succeeded most of the debt has been paid.

When Bob and Dolores started the business they became friends with a lending officer at a local bank. The business was started on "love money"—personal savings and a loan from Dolores' mother. As the business expanded Bob worked with the lending officer for bank loans.

Five years ago, the lending officer became the bank president. By then, the bank president had great confidence in Bob and Dolores and so they were able to borrow money as they needed it. Unfortunately, this situation has changed.

The local bank was acquired by a larger bank. And their friend the bank president has left.

Since Bob and Dolores would like to open up a second store, they need to borrow a considerable amount of money. The new lending officer at the bank wants more than the monthly financial statements. The whole relationship has become more formal. Bob has sensed that he will have to develop a formal business plan to convince the bank to loan them the money for the second store.

This banking crisis came to a head recently when Bob and Dolores were planning their inventory for Christmas. Typically, they would expand their loans to get extra merchandise in for their best selling season. This was so logical that the loan had become almost automatic.

However, this year the new lending officer objected. He complained that Bob and Dolores do not turn the merchandise as fast as national averages. He gave them only half the money they asked for. Bob was shocked. Ten years of good business dealings seemed to mean nothing. There were rumors that the bank was no longer interested in lending money to small businesses. Perhaps the rumors were true.

There is more to borrowing money than the numbers. When you are borrowing for a small business there is a personal relationship and mutual confidence that should be developed. The numbers are important, but character is even more important. Will you do what you say you will do? That is character. It is necessary to try things that may fail. Not every idea is a sure-fire success. If you establish a good relationship with a lender, you are allowed to fail occasionally.

(Bob and Dolores eventually found a new relationship with a banker. They also wrote their first business plan. They can get the money they need.)

As you've seen, you need some money in your pocket to operate your business and this can be a big problem if it isn't there, whether or not your business is successful. Determining if your business is successful is often a difficult financial decision and that's what we'll look at in the next chapter.

CHAPTER NINE

The Financial Decision II—Profits: How Much Money Am I Making?

Buying a Mercedes on $18,000 a year

I once had a client who owned a sales and distribution company. She was confused and worried. She had just received a profit and loss statement from her accountant and it showed that during the previous year she had a profit of only $18,000.

She was surprised and so was I. It seemed to me that she had a good little business that was making a lot more than that. She told me she had been able to buy a car last year and although it was a used car, it was a Mercedes.

We examined the profit and loss statement line by line and saw that the way her business operated, it was subject to many favorable tax interpretations. When we reworked the

"Sometimes you have to look pretty
hard to find out how the business is doing"

figures, we found that she had actually made about $60,000 in the last year. Did she have a bad accountant? No, she had a great accountant! He had saved her a bundle in taxes. But of course, she had no idea how her business was doing.

What you must decide about profits and losses

Unfortunately, many small business owners have a blind spot when it comes to understanding how to account for the money in their business. As we discussed in the last chapter, one who judges the success of a business solely on the amount of cash available will make a lot of bad decisions.

The future of a business is determined to a great extent by its profitability. If your business is very profitable you will be inclined to continue the activities that caused this happy result. If your business is operating at a loss, you will be wanting change. The profitability of each of the specific activities of the business is especially important. A profitable service could be expanded. A losing product could be dropped.

Profits and losses are not numbers written in stone and passed down from the "accounting gods." Actually, they are numbers that have to be decided by the owner, based on information gathered from company systems and accounting expertise. As you've seen with the "Mercedes" owner, you may have one profit number for tax purposes, and need totally different numbers that you can use to evaluate your business. Determining these numbers are crucial decisions in and of themselves, because they have an impact on so many other decisions.

Most small business owners don't have
the financial facts needed to make
good decisions about their businesses.

If I'm able to convince you to spend more time talking with your accountant about your business, I will have accomplished what I set out to do in this chapter.

If an owner doesn't keep good records and hire a good accountant, there won't be enough knowledge about the business to know how it's doing, let alone to make decisions about the future. What is surprising and confusing is that simply hiring a good accountant rarely improves the situation.

Most accountants <u>are</u> trained to help an owner determine how the business is doing. But that training is all too often not put to use. That's because most accountants who work with small business owners concentrate on preparing information for tax reporting and not on the statistics needed to make good business decisions.

Let's face it, taxes must be accurately reported and paid. That's the law. Unfortunately, there's no law that says that you have to know the financial facts in order to make decisions about your business. Maybe there should be.

The income tax laws contain countless rules outlining how each business transaction must be recorded in order to determine the tax to be paid. These rules are the result of political decisions by Congress after relentless lobbying by special interest groups.

Since the tax laws are based on political decisions and not business logic, they are hard to learn and apply. That's why accountants who work with small businesses often become tax specialists. And many small business owners have come to believe that the only reason they need an accountant is for taxes. To make matters worse, financial statements that owners should be able to rely on for financial facts are prepared using the tax rules. The results are misleading at best. You may not be able to recognize your own business from the financial statements. Sales, cost of sales, and expenses will probably all be different than you thought they were. Often the tax version of these numbers are worthless for decision making purposes. Most owners don't have the financial facts needed to make good decisions about their businesses.

The need for two sets of records

Susan was very positive. She had made up her mind that she needed an accountant to handle finances. "I've never understood financial statements and taxes too well," said Susan, "so I thought I'd hire an accountant to worry about them."

I asked her what she had done about financial matters and budgets when she was managing a department in the corporation. Did she leave it for the accountants to worry about?

"No," said Susan. "And I guess this should be the same. In the corporation the accountants were responsible for putting the numbers together, but I had to decide what was happening and propose how the company should spend its money. But I never had to deal with taxes or balance sheets."

Susan understood that she was going to have to be responsible for finances. There was no way she could just turn them over to somebody and walk away. I advised her to get an accountant to handle her taxes, and then I warned her that the accountant would not do much to help her understand what was going on in the business.

What I said made sense to her, but she asked, "What do I do about it?" I told her that I thought a business should have two sets of records—one for tax purposes and one for the owner to use for decision-making purposes. The latter should present the facts using good accounting practices.

"Isn't that like cheating?" Susan asked. "Having two sets of books sounds like cheating to me." I told her that it wasn't cheating. The tax laws allow many deductions which don't make good sense in evaluating the business. It is really a question of the same numbers being used for two different purposes. Cheating would be deliberately changing those numbers to understate income or overstate expenses.

(Incidentally, it really is stupid to try to cheat the government out of taxes. Cheating means you are deliberately slowing the growth of your business, and if your business succeeds, you have several problems. Short of serving three to six years in the slammer, the worst of these problems is that you won't be able to trust anyone else to handle your books for fear you'll be discovered.)

Susan then asked how she should keep two sets of books. I told her that it was actually the same set of books, but the reports would be prepared differently. I suggested that Susan use a technique I call "Alley Cat Accounting" to keep track of how she is doing and let her accountant take care of the taxes.

"Alley Cat Accounting"

The purpose of alley cat accounting is to allow a small business owner to determine profit or loss on a daily, weekly, or monthly basis without waiting for the accountant to do the books. I call it "alley cat" because it's quick and dirty. It's not intended to be accurate to the penny, nor is it intended to replace conventional accounting techniques.

Once an alley cat system has been set up, sales figures are the only information that an owner needs to determine profit or loss. A system is set up by analyzing two types of costs—cost of sales and overhead costs.

The first step in developing an alley cat system is to identify the specific direct costs associated with each type of sale. These costs should be stated as a percentage of each sale. For example, a retailer may have a direct cost of 60% on a line of merchandise. (The retailer pays $60 for the item and sells it for $100.) The gross margin is the difference between the direct cost and the selling price. In this case the gross margin would be 40%.

Alley cat accounting seeks to find out how much gross margin you earn each day. This is determined by multiplying sales by the percentage of gross margin earned on each sale. Suppose the retailer sold $800 worth of merchandise at a 40% gross margin. The retailer would have earned $320 that day.

All the costs of doing business other than those included as a direct cost of the sale might be called overhead costs. These costs should be identified and totalled for the day, month, and year.

Assume that our retail friend had overhead costs, including rent, advertising, insurance, utilities and salaries of

$50,000 per year. This would break down to $4,167 per month and assuming 24 working days, $174 a day.

Using alley cat accounting you calculate the gross margin and the overhead for the same period of time and deduct one from the other to determine your profit or loss for the period. In the example above, the $800 of sales produced $320 gross margin from which one would deduct the $174 daily overhead. That means about $146 of profit was earned that day.

Applying these ideas to Susan's case is a straightforward procedure. Susan has two types of sales. One type is where Susan does all the work herself. In the second type, she has a subcontractor do the work, and she pays the subcontractor 1/3 of what is billed to the customer.

Susan's gross margin is determined by adding all the billings based on her work and 2/3 of the billings based on the subcontractors' work. Susan deducts her overhead from the total, and the remainder is her profit (and salary as well).

Let's suppose that in one month Susan's bills are $4,000 based on her work and $2,000 of the subcontractor's work. The gross margin would be $4,000 plus (2/3 of $2,000) $1,333 to equal $5,333. If Susan's monthly overhead was $3,000, her profit would be $2,333.

Basic financial statements defined

Susan asked me to give her a refresher course on financial statements. There are two: the balance sheet and the profit and loss statement.

The balance sheet is a "snap shot" of the business on a specific day. One side of the balance sheet shows the value of the assets. Assets are items like cash, accounts receivables, inventory, equipment, buildings, and land that the business owns.

On the other side of the balance sheet are liabilities and net worth. Liabilities are items like accounts payable and notes payable which the business owes. "Net worth" is the difference between the two and identifies the balance amount which shows the value of the owner's interest in the business.

The other basic report is a "profit or loss" statement. A profit or loss statement records the operation of the business during a specific period of time. It could be a month, three months, or a year. The profit or loss statement records sales and it also records expenses. The total expenses are subtracted from the total sales, showing either a profit or a loss.

There is an interrelationship between the balance sheet and the profit or loss statement. You need to understand it in order to understand these reports in your business. This relationship is known as "double entry" bookkeeping. For example, if you pay the telephone bill, the accounting entry reduces cash (on the balance sheet) and increases telephone expenses (on the profit and loss statement).

The balance sheet and the profit or loss statements are the basic "languages" of business. You need to understand these reports in order to make good decisions as well as to communicate information to lenders or investors.

I've advised many business owners to take a book-keeping course at a local high school. Another alternative is to bug your accountant to help you.

(Susan chose to bug her accountant and me about how the finances in her business work. And we are all delighted. Susan now has the structure in place to make some good decisions.)

More "alley cat" accounting — the missing link in businesses

Although Cindy keeps meticulous records, she has never really known how her business stands. Her accountant prepares financial statements every three months, but Cindy finds it hard to relate the statements to what is going on in the business. I decided to show Cindy "alley cat" accounting.

Let's see if we can help Cindy determine her profit each month. The first step is identifying the monthly expenses that Cindy must pay regardless of how many moving jobs she does—the cost of the trucks, insurance, office rental, phone, advertising, and salaries. Let's assume that these expenses total $8,000 per month. We will call that the "overhead."

Next we need to identify the direct cost of each sale. In Cindy's case this means the cost of labor for each move. When Cindy estimates a job, she tries to establish labor costs at 1/4 the amount of the sale, but depending on how each move goes, the actual amount will vary.

Cindy already keeps records on the number of labor hours used on each job so she can easily calculate her "gross margin"—the difference between the sale and the direct cost of the sale. Let's assume that a move for which Cindy was able to charge $2,400 included $600 of labor. Cindy's gross margin on the move would be $1,800 ($2,400 less $600).

Since Cindy's monthly overhead was $8,000, it's easy to see that she needs five moves like the one described to have a profitable month. By calculating the gross margin on each job and knowing how this compares to overhead, Cindy is now able to determine where she stands at any point in time.

Alley cat accounting is the missing link for decision making in many small businesses. The purpose is to give an owner a quick fix about what is going on. It needn't be accurate to the penny. Many of the overhead costs will be based on averages. Nevertheless, Cindy was able to see the financial part of her business very clearly for the first time. She could tell how much she was losing in the slow months and gauge the benefits of taking on added capacity in the busy months.

Stop the business!

The most unusual situation of unprofitableness I can ever recall was that of some very experienced people who had started a photography company. They had priced their services based on their notion of what the price had to be to meet competition. They had made only a few sales and they were running out of money. Things were obviously not good.

When we did alley cat accounting, we made a surprising discovery. The direct cost of each service was actually exceeding the price they were charging for it—before even considering overhead.

It was necessary to stop the business and rethink it. One more sale would have put them out of business for good. It was a good thing their early sales efforts had been ineffective.

What is a profitable sale?

Applying alley cat accounting to Alex's restaurant is more difficult but still useful. One of the problems is the great variability in the percentage of gross margins to selling price of items on the menu.

For example, in a simple meal of a hot dog, french fries, and a soft drink there are very different cost factors. A hot dog that sells for $1.20 might have a food cost of .60 because of the high cost of meat. The cost of french fries, which sell for a dollar, varies according to the seasonal market price of potatoes from .30 to .50. A soft drink which sells for .60 might use only .06 worth of syrup. That's why restaurants always ask you if you'd like something to drink.

Both the industry and Alex aim to have the direct cost of food no more than 30% of sales. Whenever Alex has had accounting statements produced, the cost has always been closer to 40%. No one has ever accused Alex of running a tight ship.

But, the alley cat accounting approach has been most useful in making decisions to turn this business around. For example, when Alex changed his hours to stay open for the movie crowd, he could easily see if the move was profitable.

He knew that staying open would increase his overhead by $50 per night because of increased labor costs. He assumed 40% of his sales would be food costs which means that for every $100 in sales, $60 is gross margin. Therefore, he would be ahead if he did just $100 in sales. He immediately started to have $300 nights, so it was obviously a good move.

Alex is now reevaluating his business with alley cat accounting techniques. He's trying to evaluate each variable. For example, he is measuring dining room profits versus carryout profits. He's examining sales by day of the week, by daily specials, and by time of day. Alex's thinking is now where it should be, instead of lamenting about being overworked and underpaid for all these years. He is now concentrating on making his business succeed.

Getting information can cost money

Alley cat accounting does have its limitations. When I first started working with Bob and Dolores, I innocently asked the question, "What is a profitable day?" Bob started talking about various sales promotions, so I rephrased the question: "How much do you have to sell in a day to break even?" They also avoided answering that question.

Bob and Dolores were acting as if it was confidential information they didn't want to reveal. As I pressed the issue, I discovered that they didn't know the answer. So with some quick alley cat accounting we were able to give them an idea of what they needed to do each day. They keep track of sales and by figuring out average margins for each department, we were able to get a rough idea of the daily sales required.

While knowing this information was valuable, it was not enough information on which to base the decisions that would truly make this store successful. In a retail operation, inventory is what the business is all about, and we didn't have control of inventory. Taking a physical inventory was a massive, expensive job which Bob and Dolores did twice a year. But it usually took three months to get the inventory calculated and another three months for the accountants to get statements together. The information was therefore never timely or useful for making decisions. From the purchasing side, many reordering decisions were made by guess work and many out-of-stock items were never reordered.

Having information costs money. In a small business it is always necessary to evaluate how much money you should spend to get more information. That's why "alley cat" procedures are useful. They are both low-cost and very effective. But sometimes more information is needed. Bob and Dolores represent an example of such a time.

(Bob and Dolores decided that the business would not grow unless they gained control over their inventory. The answer was a computerized point-of-sale system which produced timely inventory records and also helped with purchasing. This was a good investment and has eliminated a lot of the guesswork.)

Understanding finances will improve decisions

Because of Jim's accounting background, Jim and Mike have always had a good handle on their financial situation. Their systems could serve as a model for many small businesses. They maintain a bookkeeping system that enables their accountant to prepare monthly statements. These include: a profit and loss statement, a balance sheet, and an aging statement for the accounts receivable.

Jim tries to explain the profit or loss each month. He studies the statement and comes up with the answers. It's usually a fluctuation in sales that causes the difference in profits. An extra weekly pay day is also a common reason for profit to be down. The purpose of these monthly reviews is to keep the business under control.

The aging statements identify how much past due accounts receivables are on the books. Studying this statement often leads Jim to get on the phone and talk to a customer whose bill is overdue.

Jim prepares his own cash flow analysis sheet. Using a large calendar, he pre-identifies events that will involve cash payments like rent, payrolls, and taxes. He estimates other receipts and payments so he has a running prediction of his bank balance for the next few weeks. Using this system, Jim rarely has to act in panic over cash.

Jim also does his own alley cat accounting. He records daily production totals by product line. He has estimated the gross margin on each product so he knows what is a break-even day and what is a profitable day. This has been a most useful tool in production planning.

Both raw material and finished goods inventory records are now on the computer, so Jim is able to produce inventory reports as needed. This has improved the purchasing function and also has made the profit and loss statement more accurate.

What I have just described is a company that gives far more attention to the figures than most small businesses ever dream of doing. Obviously, the reason for this is that Jim has a background as an accountant. He uses these numbers as tools to understand his business. Actually, I've only mentioned about half of what he does. He also has all kinds of special analysis reports and charts that he works up. Is this overkill? Is Jim too obsessed with the numbers?

Jim and Mike have a very profitable business. They make numerous good decisions. They have many facts to use to make these decisions. Having these facts is part of their management style. It works for them.

How many facts you need to have available about your business in order to make good decisions is, in itself, a crucial decision. As we have seen in this chapter, an owner who tries to run a business using only the check book balance is highly at risk.

Above all, make sure that you review and understand any financial report on your business. Jim and Mike are able to relate the decisions they make about their business to the numbers and vice versa. This is what makes them so effective. The numbers are simply the easiest way to understand the effect of your decisions. Sometimes they are the only way. So don't sell yourself short. If you think you don't understand finances, then refocus your attention. Study the subject until you do understand. Check with your accountant, the high school business teachers, or the local library. It will pay off—I promise.

CHAPTER TEN

The Capacity Decision:
I Must Be Successful Because
I Can't Handle Any More Business

Success means figuring out how to expand capacity

I have a sure-fire way to pick a fight at a party. In response to the question, "How's business?", there are always people who boast that they are so busy they could not possibly handle any new work. At first this sounds like success. When people are pounding their chests with such a story, we probably tend to envy them. In truth, these proud business owners are admitting that they haven't figured out how to expand capacity. They've made bad business decisions. Of course, if you express this at a party you'd better make sure the braggarts aren't bigger than you are.

By definition, "small business" means limited capacity. The success of a business is often determined by the

"Sometimes you have too many hats to wear."

owner's ability to expand that capacity. The obstacles to expansion change as a business grows. The most common blocks to increasing capacity are money, employees, supervision, space, systems, and equipment. Typically, an owner gets enough money and then has trouble finding the right employees. Just when the right employees appear, an owner runs out of space. The problem of capacity is continuous and has a "changing face" in any growing business.

Excess capacity is a terrific marketing tool

Running out of capacity does imply some success. It means products or services are being sold. But sales efforts that have to be stopped when capacity is reached and then restarted will not be as effective as those that are continuing. Marketing and capacity, have a direct—and surprising—relationship. I first witnessed this years ago when a one-truck delivery company became a two-truck company.

The trucking company was a profitable little business with only one truck. However, the truck was getting very old and in need of a major overhaul. The owner planned to buy a new truck as well as fix up the old one, hoping that he could increase his business enough to pay for the new truck. We put together a sound marketing plan to increase business. But the plan was never implemented because the business increased so fast there wasn't time.

There are two questions a customer commonly asks: "How much?" and "When?" When the answer to the "when" question means fast service, price is often secondary. It turned out that the trucking company had a second truck's worth of business just waiting for the available space. The business doubled overnight.

Was this an isolated incident? I don't think so. I've seen numerous cases where capacity was expanded and business increased to the new capacity before any new marketing was done. Having excess capacity can greatly help your marketing.

The "Buying Yourself a Job" stage

At first capacity seemed like a remote issue to Susan. "My concern is making enough sales to have this business survive," said Susan. This attitude is common in someone starting a business. The major issue is buying oneself a job. Capacity is looked at in terms of "my" capacity—"How much can I do?" This is an employee mentality rather than one of an owner. An owner's approach is getting more customers and doing more for them. Satisfied customers mean success.

Some business owners never get past the "buying yourself a job" stage. This is especially common in professional practices and in the skilled trades where a business is operated by a "lone wolf." The resulting lack of capacity artificially restricts the natural growth of the business and consequently frustrates the owner.

Changing from a one-person operation to having associates and helpers is a trauma to many business owners. There is a certain degree of comfort in doing it all yourself. That way it gets done "right," or at least in the way that you want it done.

Normally the first helpers in a business will be doing

the more routine functions, which should free up the owner's time. Many owners resist taking on these helpers for reasons I've never been able to determine. In some cases, I suspect the owner likes to do the routine. The strongest argument for hiring helpers is to identify how much a good helper will be paid. Usually it is such a modest amount that the owner will quickly realize that he or she shouldn't be spending time that's already in short supply on the routine tasks a helper can do.

For example, a young client who was planning to open a restaurant told me that he planned to spend all his time working hard waiting on customers. He quickly realized that this was not a good use of his time if he could hire waiters for about the minimum wage.

What do we need to expand next?

Sometimes the key business decision is identifying the next new job that will increase capacity. For example, in most retail operations it's logical to add more clerks to serve the customer. But in certain types of businesses more clerks may spell disaster. One good example is the repair business. The most important part of such a business is to determine what should be accepted for repair. Therefore, the owner or someone very experienced has to deal with the customer.

The model for many small businesses is the owner who operates and supervises all areas of the business and has many helpers, each of whom does a specific job. Such a business will typically grow to the owner's capacity to supervise and once that limit is reached, capacity is reached.

Expanding capacity means taking on someone to perform the owner's management functions and that may have to be a partner. Many owners stop growth at this point. The business will become static until something happens either to the owner or the market place.

Biting off more than you can chew

Susan had to face the issue of capacity at a very early stage of her business. A large company asked her to submit a proposal on a big project. It was a computer design project that would have required the efforts of five or six people for a year. After reviewing the space, equipment, and supervision required to do this project successfully, Susan decided not to bid. When I asked her why she made this decision, she replied, "I wasn't ready."

What a difficult decision this was for Susan! She could have gone from a start-up business to a company doing several hundred thousand dollars per year—based on just one deal. But Susan had extensive experience in her field. She knew the project would be difficult without an experienced organization behind her. She knew all her time would be tied up for a year while supervising the project. This isn't the direction she wanted for her business. She could look beyond the project and see that once it was done she would have to start her business all over again, something like falling off a cliff.

I've worked with many clients who were confronted with the opportunity to get a very large piece of business at a very early stage. Some decided to do the work and some of them made a lot of money. But every one of them had many problems adjusting their businesses after the major sale.

Unfortunately, biting off more than you can chew can be a prelude to disaster. The classic case was that of the owner of a start-up remodeling company who decided to take on a large apartment complex. The project began with excitement and promise. As time passed, little things started to go wrong. Workers didn't show up; equipment didn't function.

The job was originally scheduled to be done in two months. But, after two months they had barely scratched the surface. Everything they had touched turned to dust. That company's first job was its last job. The only thing that saved the owner from bankruptcy was walking away from the job after six months. If he hadn't, he might still be struggling.

Capacity has to be realistically assessed. Don't let greed get in the way. Not being able to do the job can backfire on you in ways you'd never dream. On the other hand, if you're going to be successful, you'll need to continually assess capacity and each increase involves some risk. But, so does getting up in the morning. Capacity decisions are the toughest, but I think Susan made her first one correctly.

Being realistic about the state of your capabilities can pay many dividends. As it turned out, Susan earned considerable respect by turning down the large job. Her erstwhile clients began to question how they had defined the project. Perhaps they were trying to do too much all at once, and they could be devising a plan for failure. Ultimately, they settled on several small projects instead of the large one. Susan did have a role in one of the projects and it was one that she could handle effectively.

The seasonal business

For all practical purposes, Cindy has two businesses. During the winter months she is like the washing machine repairman of television fame, lonely and bored and waiting for the phone to ring. But in the spring and fall, Cindy and her crew are running at full speed trying to handle the available business.

Most seasonal businesses try to even out the seasons to match capacity. Sometimes this is done successfully. Landscapers shovel snow; bike shops rent skis. But for most seasonal businesses the off months are a big headache, and that is the case with Cindy.

If families don't want to move during the winter, there is nothing Cindy can do to entice them into it. Moving something other than families would be the likely prescription, and Cindy has a contract with an appliance store to move refrigerators, stoves, etc.

Another common alternative is to decide that the off season is like pushing water uphill and to forget it, concentrating instead on building the business during the "on" season. Why can't Cindy rent a number of trucks and hire a bunch of musclemen during the season and just forget about the winter? It was such a good idea I tried it out on Cindy.

"I do rent some trucks and hire some extra people," said Cindy, "but that doesn't solve my problem of having enough <u>experienced</u> leaders." It turns out that the moving business requires more brains than brawn. At least brains are the commodity which is in shortest supply.

If one moves in the spring during the busy season, the crew will likely consist of one experienced mover and a bunch of weight lifters. The experienced mover probably won't even spend much time in your home, because he is concentrating on getting the truck loaded properly. However, if you should move in the winter, the full crew is probably very experienced. (We all have mysteries from our childhood. One I harbored for many years was why the movers called the little guy in from the truck to put the refrigerator on his back and carry it down the stairs. Now I know that he was the only one who knew how to do it without knocking down a wall.)

Cindy's situation illustrates how important it is for an owner to understand capacity problems. If all the other capacity questions can be readily answered, then the issue of experienced leaders is one that a successful business must face. It means giving special attention to identifying and training leaders. It certainly means that we should try to keep these experienced people employed all year. That puts a new value on having at least some winter business.

The basic conflict is a common one. It's capacity versus maintaining good service. Without an experienced leader, a household move becomes a high-risk venture. Furniture will be broken. Workers will be injured. Cindy's reputation for quality service will suffer. It may not even be profitable because inexperienced workers may be too slow. The limits of the business are clearly established unless Cindy works on ways to find more experienced leaders.

Expanding capacity must include maintaining quality

As soon as I hear that a restaurant has opened, I plan to try it out right away. That's because I have a theory that a restaurant is as good as its ever going to be soon after it opens. This is the stage where there is no capacity problem, and the owner's full attention is on the details of the food and service. I've experienced good food and wonderful attentive service during these "honeymoon" periods. I look forward to going back and becoming a regular customer.

Most often, it's a capacity problem disguised as success that stops a restaurant from being successful. A restaurant reporter from a local newspaper will come by and try out the eatery. The reporter will write about his or her experiences, probably favorably. People will read the article and decide to dine at this new place. Suddenly, lines form—business is great. The new restaurant is a gold mine. The owner is convinced that he will become a millionaire, maybe even a billionaire!

After about two months, the lines begin to thin. And after six months the owner starts to get lonely. After two years the restaurant quietly goes out of business with the owner lamenting, "If only the newspaper would print another article."

What goes wrong in these cases? It is a scenario that is repeated countless times. Basically, it's a capacity problem. When the crowds come, the restaurant can't maintain the high-quality food or service. As a result, most of those who try out the restaurant after reading the article are not impressed—at least not impressed enough to come back. And to make matters worse, the "regular" clientele, those who are naturally attracted to the place, become unhappy because of the crowds and they stop coming.

When I told Alex this story, he asked me how I knew that had happened to him. I told him that the story would be the same for any business whose quality of service or products had slipped. This does happen often, especially in the restaurant business, because each meal becomes a test. The customers will decide—meal by meal—if they want to come back. Every meal served is important.

Building on something that works

By now, both breakfast and after-the-movie business at Alex's was brisk. On some days people had to wait in line during those times. But lunch and dinner had not improved much. The place was still almost empty. Alex wanted to get more patrons for these meals, but he had been trying to do that for years.

It's usually easier to build on something that is already working than it is to fix something that is broken. It wasn't clear that Alex could ever build a successful lunch and dinner business in this location. We would continue to try, but I thought our major focus should be on further expanding breakfast and after-the-movie business. This would mean expanding capacity by adding help and perhaps adding to the menu, particularly for the movie crowd, with some fast-food items such as ice cream "creations." I also thought more seats should be added.

There is one sure way to attract Alex's attention, and

that is to suggest that he spend some money. Alex believed that the breakfast and after-the-movie time segments were going perfectly. He had never been so profitable. Now, if anything, he argued he should be spending money to promote lunch and supper.

Alex was able to present his arguments very powerfully, and he was a very stubborn person once he took a stand. On the other hand, he was not considering the situation from his customer's point of view. We knew that both in the morning and during the late evening there were many potential customers passing the restaurant. Most likely they were in a hurry. They didn't want to stand in line and they would appreciate fast service. If they had a good experience they would come back. It was this last point that allowed me to convince Alex to increase capacity. I agreed that lunch and supper needed to be promoted, and I argued that the best way to promote those meals was to encourage existing customers to try lunch and supper. The more customers he had for breakfast and after-the-movies, the better his chances of enticing them into the restaurant at other times.

Alex agreed to increase capacity. As you might imagine, business at breakfast and during the late evening increased immediately and continued to grow. The more attention that he put into those two times of day, the more people stopped in to eat with Alex. Alas, it's still lonely at lunch and supper, but Alex doesn't have to spend nearly as much time with bill collectors any more. The business has turned the corner toward prosperity.

When is a shelf really full?
The hidden capacity

One of the standard truisms of the retail industry is: You can't sell from an empty shelf. The underlying problem is trying to determine whether a shelf is full or empty.

I have a number of clients who are distributors, that is they supply goods to retailers. They find that they must continually follow up on their retail accounts to get reorders, even if the merchandise is selling well.

One of my distributor clients tells the story of stopping in to see several retail accounts he had not had contact with for about six months. In every case he was unable to find any of his merchandise in the store. When he asked the store managers about this, almost every one praised the products and said that they sold quickly. When he asked why they weren't reordered, nobody knew the answer. Each thought the products should have been restocked. This story points up the crucial role of purchasing in a retail store.

"It's a real guessing game at times," said Dolores. "It often seems that the goods that sell the best take the longest to reorder. And of course, you never know for sure what's going to sell quickly."

"I think Dolores has super instincts about what to buy," said Bob. "She's being overly modest. But, we try to be very careful to not over order, because we tend to live with our mistakes for a long time."

Bob's belief that he must live with goods that don't sell bothers me. That approach leads to clogging the shelves with slow moving merchandise and that is the same as having empty shelves. This pattern also fits with the banker's complaint that Bob and Dolores didn't turn their inventory quickly enough. Inventory turns are determined by dividing total sales by average inventory. The result is a number which can be used to gauge and compare how efficiently the inventory is turning over—being sold.

I asked Bob and Dolores how they got rid of their mistakes. They said they had a clearance sale twice a year, one after Christmas and a side-walk sale in the summer. But they agreed that they should get more aggressive in turning the merchandise.

One of the most successful retailers I've seen was in the furniture business. The owners had a preplanned turn-over policy. Sell it within a given period or put it on sale. If the item still didn't sell, it was drastically reduced, and after that it was taken to an auctioneer or given away to charity. The moral of this story is: Don't dwell on mistakes. Get rid of the mistakes so you can focus on what sells well.

The computerized inventory control system which Bob and Dolores had purchased helped them get an idea about the size of their inventory, but they were not using it as part of their purchasing procedure yet. I asked them how they did their purchasing.

"It depends on the item," said Dolores. "The staples we keep in stock all the time are reordered as soon as the stock is low. The other things we usually order when the salesman calls."

It was clear that much of the purchasing was done without regard to how well the items had previously sold, except for what information Bob or Dolores might remember. This was an area where the inventory control system might help them. Memory can fade fast. It's not unusual for several items to be ordered and one of them turn out to be so popular that it immediately sells out. If the popular item can be identified and reordered, sales can be increased <u>tremendously</u>.

I think the universal rule in retailing should be: Sell from a shelf that contains items your customers have shown they want to buy. It isn't enough to just fill up the shelves.

By identifying what sold quickly, Bob and Dolores were able to adjust their purchasing accordingly. Within a year, sales increased to nearly the equivalent of having a second store. This old established business is now growing faster than its discount-minded competitors. It's a case of having the capacity to meet the customer's needs. This capacity is hidden to a retailer who doesn't quickly identify what his customers buy.

Growing pains (and joys)

Mike and Jim had a new twist. They had been trying to expand their business so that their one big customer, Mr. Retailer, would not be so important. But now an opportunity arose (or perhaps it was an ultimatum) to accept even more business from Mr. Retailer.

Mr. Retailer had decided to reduce the number of suppliers that manufactured games. Mike and Jim had a chance to make some similar games. There was some hint that this was a direct competition and that one manufacturer would take all, but Mike and Jim concentrated on winning and they did. (Losing could have put them out of business.)

It wasn't clear just how much new business they would be getting from Mr. Retailer, but it appeared their business might increase 50 to 100%. Doubling the business—that's a lot of games!

I asked about capacity, and Mike and Jim appeared calm enough. They thought they had enough space and they had some extra machinery that was not being used. They also knew another manufacturer to whom they could subcontract part of the operation. Mike and Jim would need to add some employees, but they had plenty of time to get them trained. Both decided they would devote most of their time in the next six months to supervising the very profitable operation. Other marketing efforts would need to take a back seat.

The production of the new items was to coincide with the release of one of Mr. Retailers seasonal catalogues. It appeared that this large increase in business would be handled very smoothly.

All hell broke loose when the first order from Mr. Retailer arrived. The order called for Mike and Jim to produce—within the next month—almost three times more than they had ever produced in 30 days. The panic caused by this first order had not subsided when two weeks later, a second order of about the same size arrived.

Mike and Jim began working 18 hours a day 7 days a week. They started hiring employees. They got the contract manufacturer going and they brought the old machinery out of moth balls. They increased production, but not enough to make a dent in the orders.

It seemed that whatever could go wrong, did. The contract manufacturer turned out to be disorganized and the workmanship was not reliable, so the sub-contracting was of little help. Reliable employees were hard to find. Mike, Jim and their plant manager spent endless hours hiring and training, but the new employees were not yet very productive. Furthermore, some of the old equipment didn't work very well.

Management at Mr. Retailer was unhappy because their orders were not being filled. They keep score and any vendor who falls below 90% in order fulfillment is in trouble. Mike and Jim were at 75% and less and were hearing plenty about it. However, it was a two-way street. It became obvious that someone at Mr. Retailer had goofed and delayed too long in placing the initial orders. Mike and Jim hoped that this would be remembered when their account was reviewed.

It took five months but production finally started to catch up. Orders started to slow down, and by then Mike and Jim had a much more experienced workforce. But, both of them were near exhaustion.

Then the unthinkable happened. Mr. Retailer declared that they had much too much inventory of Mike and Jim's games. They stopped placing new orders. Jim and Mike had to decide if they should produce for inventory, although there were no new orders. They decided they should, but they were limited by how much space they had to store the games.

Now Mr. Retailer's management was unhappy because they had too much inventory. We are beginning to suspect that Mr. Retailer's "state of the art" system of inventory control isn't quite what management thinks it is.

Does having capacity mean we are able to stay on the roller coaster? There are some peaks and valleys in every business but few have to go through what Mike and Jim have gone through. There was compensation, however. There were record sales and record profits as well as record distress and pain.

"It may not be easy to measure
the performance of your employees."

CHAPTER ELEVEN

The Personnel Decisions:
Why Can't Employees Be More Like Us?

It's hard to clone yourself

Because a small business is just that—small, each employee has a significant impact on the business. Good personnel decisions can make your business succeed beyond your wildest dreams, because you'll have productive employees to help you. These decisions involve hiring, training, motivating, supervising, and compensating employees.

Personnel decisions are harder to make than they may first appear to be because there is a big difference between you and your employees. That fact is often not obvious. The differences are found in attitude, viewpoint, and commitment. Many owners are surprised and disappointed when employees act like employees.

Committed owners believe they are building teams and that their employees, the team members, should share the same goals that they, as owners, do. What many owners overlook is the fact that each employee will have a set of overriding goals unrelated to his or her employment. For example, employees like to know the specific duties of the job, how to please the boss, the pay and expected hours of work. The owner's goals may have to do with cash flow, production schedules, and wooing new customers. So, there is built-in conflict. It can surface, for example, when an otherwise "good" employee leaves at the normal quitting time. I've heard "workaholic" owners question the loyalty of such employees—those don't put in the same insane hours they do.

No matter how hard you try, your employees will not be clones of you. They may possess more skills, but they will not have your commitment or attitude toward the business. Once you begin to recognize that there is an employee's point of view, you are on your way to making good personnel decisions.

90% of new hires are the best they're going to be on the day you hire them

Susan Andrews had just recently hired her first employee. I remember how excited she was. She had found the perfect fit. Now she had a colleague to work with her, and it would mean more profit for the business as well.

Susan had taken on a large project that included developing a computer system. She decided that the best way to do this project was to find someone who was a computer expert to do much of the detail work. She put the word out to some of her friends that she was looking for such a helper and, like magic, Veronica appeared.

Veronica had been a computer programmer in a large corporation for a number of years. She had left that job to go back to school for a Masters degree. She was trying to support herself as a freelance programmer and Susan's opportunity fit into her plans. Susan was able to pay her top dollar for 20 hours of work per week, and Susan would still have a handsome profit on the transaction. Moreover, Veronica had specific experience doing just this type of project. Susan thought that she would even hire Veronica full time after her graduation. Perhaps Veronica would even be a partner in the firm one day.

How lucky! Susan had needed to talk to only one person and she found someone who was going to be an instant success. Susan set aside a couple of weeks to train Veronica on the way she wanted things done. The first work that Veronica did was somewhat flawed. But Susan rationalized that this was all part of the learning process, and she set up more training sessions.

It took Susan about two months to discover that Veronica was so slow that there was no way that her time could be charged to the project. Even with the mark-up, Veronica's pay was more than Susan could collect from the client. It was also evident that Veronica had some bad habits, one being that her work products were sloppy and lacked organization. Worst of all, she didn't seem to listen; whatever Susan said was summarily ignored.

What had started out as such a promising venture had become a nightmare. After three months Susan let Veronica go. Susan did a lot of soul searching to reach that decision. She felt guilty, yet she also thought that she had been burned. "Where did I go wrong?" "What could I have done differently?", she asked.

I have a theory, based on my own experiences, that 90% of the time people are the best that they're ever going to be on the day that you hire them. And 10% of the time people will turn out better than you expected when you hired them. You almost never end up getting exactly what you expected. There are good reasons for this.

The resume and interview system of hiring is imperfect at best. The prospective employee is always trying very hard to "accentuate the positive." Therefore, it should not be surprising that most people will not perform as well as you originally thought they would.

Some tips on hiring

Anything you can do in the hiring process to help you determine future performance will save you a lot of grief. Once you've determined a high probability that the prospect can do the job, you should decide the equally important question of compatibility. Do you like this person? As the owner of a small business you probably spend a lot of time around your employees, so why hire someone that you don't like? But on the other hand, be careful about hiring someone just because you like them.

It's also helpful to do some objective testing for any skills that the job requires. If the job requires typing, have the applicants type. If the job requires reading, writing, and counting, give them a brief test. There are books in the library on preparing for civil service tests. They will give you ideas for developing appropriate tests. Simple testing of skills has saved my clients enormous amounts of time and effort in tne hiring process and beyond because they quickly screen out unqualified prospects.

Another procedure which should be a standard part of your hiring process is checking references to try to determine the quality of past performances. While this is not a very reliable method of checking the quality of work, it does verify the applicant's story of dates and places. I think you'll find it well worth the time you spend doing it.

We all ultimately develop our own interviewing methods. One of the points that I like to check out in the interview is whether the applicant listens to me. This is based on my experience that an employee who doesn't listen is going to cause a lot of problems, and I might get a clue about this during the interview.

Another technique I use is to deliberately postpone a hiring decision until the next day. I've learned that I'm a born optimist and that I will focus on an applicant's positive points during an interview. It's almost as if I'm trying to convince myself of a person's merits. After the interview, the negative reasons start coming to the surface. If I'm still excited about an applicant the next morning, I'll make an offer.

But the biggest problem could be you

While having an experience like Susan had with Veronica is traumatic and likely to make you cautious in future hiring procedures, employees are rarely associated with gloom and doom. Ninety percent may not be as good as you thought they were, but that doesn't mean that most of them will be bad enough to fire. Most will be acceptable but just not the superstars that you thought they would be. In fact, after the business hires its first key employee, the owner often becomes a bigger problem than the employee. George was a good example.

George owned a print design business. It started as a "buy yourself a job" business. George operated it all by himself. He did the work, sold the product, and swept the floor. He made himself a nice living and then George decided to expand the business by hiring another print designer to do what he did.

It looked like a good move because George had lots of business. George trained the new designer and closely supervised the work. The new designer did a good job and turned out to be very productive. George was quite relieved. He had been working long hours for many years and now he had a productive employee. It was a good feeling.

The good feeling lasted until George saw his next profit and loss statement. His profit was reduced by the amount that the new designer was being paid. It was easy to see what had happened. The new employee had worked out fine but George hadn't. In effect, George had gone on vacation. He had stopped producing. Once George got going again, the business grew and became even more successful.

I have seen this same pattern repeat itself many times. The employee works out fine but the business doesn't improve because the owner goes "on vacation." Any time you hire that first key employee to do what you do, there's no doubt that you'll do your best to get that employee productive, but you'd better make sure you redefine your job as well.

Using subcontractors to grow

Susan was faced with quite a dilemma. Since she was doing business with big companies, each project she got was large enough to take a good chunk of her time. It was obvious she needed employees to help her. The problem was that she couldn't afford to hire employees until she got the additional business, and once a project ended she might have to let the employee go. At the same time, she needed very talented people with some specific skills. I asked Susan what kind of work she expected the employee to do.

"That's part of the problem," said Susan. "There are many different needs to fill—someone to sell and to be a manager and someone to do the technical work. I also need help with clerical work."

Although Susan had been doing all the work herself, it was clear that she needed to hire people with different skills. Their compensation would be quite different too. It was entirely possible that some or all of these people would not be employees, not technically at least.

Many times, the ideal way to grow a business is by using subcontractors. A subcontractor is a business or a person you hire to do a specific job. It could be a person with a secretarial service. He or she types letters for many businesses. Or it could be a person who manages a project for a fee. This is the ideal way for Susan to get the perfect people to work on each project. Such an arrangement is the "norm" in many businesses. For example, the construction industry gets most of its work done by having general contractors use subcontractors. Susan is acting like a general contractor on many of her projects because many different skills will be necessary to complete the work.

The only real downside to this approach to expanding the business is the lack of qualified subcontractors. If people are not available, often the only solution is to hire and train them yourself. Developing a network of people with skills in your line of business is all important. Susan's membership in several associations is paying off because she knows so many people in the field.

Depending on your niche in a particular field, you could be acting both as a general contractor and as a subcontractor. For example, a large consulting company had begun a gigantic project and approached Susan to do part of it. So Susan herself is acting as a subcontractor on that particular job.

One should take special care not to hire someone as a subcontractor when this person should be an employee. Since there is no withholding of payroll taxes for a subcontractor, the Internal Revenue Service takes a dim view of these arrangements. The IRS issues a set of guidelines to distinguish between an employee and a subcontractor. This is an area that should be discussed with your attorney or accountant.

Defining business relationships

Susan was able to find three people who fit her needs. Jerry was a salesman who sold personnel testing services to large corporations. He would also sell Susan's consulting services on commission. Susan had met Jerry at a meeting of a personnel association she belonged to.

Peggy had recently retired from her job as a secretary. She agreed to help Susan with clerical duties on a part time basis. Peggy was the mother-in-law of a close friend of Susan's.

Cliff was a technical expert in the benefits field. Like Susan he had previously been employed in a large corporation and had been laid off. Cliff would do a lot of the consulting services. Susan had found Cliff by placing a want ad in a trade magazine.

Susan was building quite a team. I asked her what arrangements she had made with each of them. "That's a problem," said Susan. "Cliff wants to be a partner in the business. He's had a lot of experience and it looks like he'll be able to churn out a large quantity of work and I'll make a lot of money. But I'm just not sure."

After being burned by Veronica, Susan is being very cautious about rushing into relationships. That's a well-learned lesson. Susan and I discussed what goes into making a partnership.

From the prospective of an established business owner, there are only three reasons why you might be willing to make an employee a partner. The first reason is money. The new partner could buy into the business. A second reason is a demonstrated ability to bring in a substantial amount of new business. A third reason might be the ability to help you develop other people that can do what you do. Good performance is not enough to justify making someone a partner. The skills to either increase the business by selling or expand the capacity by managing people are what Susan should expect from Cliff, in addition to his technical expertise, before she considers making him a partner.

"I'm not really sure I want a partner," said Susan. "Maybe I should encourage Cliff to do some selling to demonstrate that he should become a partner."

I advised Susan not to do that. If Cliff could both sell and do the work, he might decide that he doesn't need Susan. If that happens, Susan will have created a competitor rather than a partner. A more logical career path for Cliff in Susan's company would be as a manager and developer of other employees.

A successful sales person is very valuable to a company. But sales persons who are in a position to develop personal loyalties that might influence customers to follow them should they leave your employ have become like partners whether you wanted them to or not. This is another reason why an owner should always have final sales responsibilities and should be keeping close tabs on the sales staff.

The arrangement to have Jerry sell Susan's services seems very attractive. Obviously a sales person like Jerry who already has contact with the right people should be more effective in presenting Susan's services than someone starting out cold. Jerry won't really be an employee. He'll be an independent contractor who will be paid only when he sells something. But Jerry has not yet sold anything for Susan.

The problem with having a sales person in Jerry's situation is that most of his income will be coming from selling other things. Susan may not be very high on his priority list. She will need to make a special effort to stay in touch and keep him active and involved and thinking about her services.

You should never assume that people will respond by doing what is logically in their best interests. This is especially true with a sales person on commission. No matter how talented the sales person might be, sales management is still needed to get best results. As the owner, you will find yourself in the position of being sales manager by default. If you accept this role and manage the sales force or find someone else who will, your selling effort will be more successful.

Susan's plan to have Peggy handle the clerical chores seemed like a good idea. Peggy was known to be both trustworthy and skilled. Working part-time would be ideal for Peggy and fits Susan's budget too.

When Peggy left for two weeks to visit her daughter, Susan understood. When Peggy went on a three week camping trip, Susan understood again. What Susan had failed to understand was that retirement is often a full-time job. It almost always takes priority over work. If people want to work, they will not be retired. Having Peggy do clerical work was a good idea, but it just didn't pan out.

Susan had better luck with Cliff. Cliff is happily working on one of Susan's projects and he is earning quite a profit for Susan. As it turned out, he really didn't want the responsibility of being a partner. For the time being that issue is at rest.

Building a team

Cindy Sorrento is a very organized business owner. She runs her moving business by using systems and procedures that she has developed step by step. Since Cindy has never moved a stick of furniture herself, her personnel decisions totally define how well her moving company will function.

Cindy has four key employees, Oscar, Elmer and Robert, all experienced movers, and Rita who is an experienced packer. Cindy was very surprised to find out that she was the first mover in the area to employ women as packers. It became the subject of a very complimentary article in a local paper.

During the moving season, Oscar, Elmer, and Robert each lead a crew of movers, and Rita goes from job to job supervising the packers. During the off season, Cindy's problem is keeping them all productive because she is absolutely committed to paying these four year around.

Cindy would like to have more employees like these four. The amount of business she can handle is limited by the number of skilled employees she has. There are two constraints on hiring more people. First, employees like these are hard to find. Second, Cindy must be prepared to pay them during the slow times in order to have them when she needs them. Finding the really excellent person is the hardest part of the problem. If Cindy were to find a prospective employee she thought was perfect, she would hire him or her and then figure out some way to pay the salary.

Cindy hires a lot of helpers and most of them are new each year. This makes it crucial for Cindy to find sources of qualified help. When you need many employees to run your business, it's safe to assume that there will be turn over. Like Cindy, you will need to have a source for employees or a system to find them.

Some businesses rely totally on the "word of mouth" system. Let your friends, neighbors, and customers know what kind of help you are looking for. A little sign on a community bulletin board might help. Some businesses rely primarily on newspaper ads or employment agencies.

Cindy has a unique source—football coaches. Cindy cultivates a nodding acquaintance with all the local high school and college football coaches. She is looking for the students with both brains and brawn. She is especially interested in their reputation for responding to training as well as their work habits and reliability.

The football coaches like Cindy's jobs. They are able to tell their students about a good paying summer job that can help keep them in shape. The coaches are also well aware that if they send Cindy their problem players, they will ruin this source of good jobs for future students. Cindy gets the cream of the crop every season. She hired an all state quarterback on one of her crews.

Once she hires a summer helper, Cindy's attitude is more what one might expect from a college professor than the owner of a moving company. She has a well-developed training program, with the major stress on safety. Cindy wants no injuries, and nothing broken. So there is instruction on how to lift along with various packing and moving procedures. Common problems are identified, and there is specific emphasis on the proper manner in talking with clients because moving is traumatic for everyone. Cindy even has a dress code for her employees. She believes it is important to establish the professional image of the company.

Each moving crew is identified as a team. One of the experienced employees is the team leader and is the boss on each job. There are team goals for each move which are clearly spelled out to each team member. The goals always begin with no injuries and nothing broken. There is competition between teams and an injury or damaged furniture will be a big setback to the team. The other goals involve the time spent and details on how the move was handled. Each move is evaluated by the team leader and by Cindy. The equipment and the dress code is also inspected daily and a grade assessed.

Cindy believes that the teamwork and competition help to assure interested and involved employees. Her outstanding safety record supports her theory. Cindy's teamwork competition is great for morale and it is also reflected in her employees' pay checks. There is incentive bonus pay for each quality move. There is additional pay for the team that performs the best each month. The team leaders are paid an annual bonus based on the performance of their teams and the profits of the company.

Cindy complains that keeping track of all these numbers makes her feel like a bookkeeper, but she also believes it is a crucial part of her business. She is tracking and rewarding the employee performance which will enable the company to do an outstanding job. It's the kind of system that pays off for everyone—Cindy, her employees, and her customers.

Defining the owner's job

The first impression that most people have of Alex is that he is busy—very, very busy. He is always in motion, wiping off a table, working the cash register, or refilling a coffee cup. He's been that way as long as I've known him. I always thought it was his way of burning off nervous energy until I asked him about it.

"The reason I host, cashier, and waitress," said Alex, "is to save money. If I didn't do all this I'd have to hire an extra waitress."

I was flabbergasted to hear Alex make that statement. I knew that he was way behind in doing many of the things he needed to do to manage the business properly. I asked him how much time he thought he spent taking the place of a waitress or waiter.

"Probably about half my day." Alex confessed. "It's full time around meals."

That didn't make sense. Waiters and waitresses earn about the minimum wage and Alex's time just has to be worth more than the minimum wage. That's the type of decision you might call a "no brainer." It doesn't really matter what else Alex chooses to do with his time. He'd be better off going home to take a nap. At least he'd be better rested. The reluctance to hire a badly needed employee is a common mistake. I see it a lot in businesses that were started as one person operations. The owner did it all and still seems to want to do it all. The use of computers has made this possible in some circumstances. But mostly, these owners are wasting their own time by not hiring out the repetitive tasks. The owners need to redefine their jobs to become more productive.

Some owners don't value their own time properly. They consider their time free. An owner of a small machine shop ran the equipment himself during many hours of the week. In his mind, he was earning $75 per hour because that's what his company charged for this work. But the work could have been done by a $10 per hour employee so the owner was only earning $10 an hour while he wondered why his business was failing.

Management is what makes a company succeed and management's time is precious. Your time is worth far more than you think. I once helped some roofers analyze their business. They wanted to know if they should spend their time actually working on the roof which would replace the $20 per hour they would have to pay an employee. The alternative was to concentrate on marketing and doing more proposals to get additional business. This is an easy decision if a business intends to prosper. The success of the business would be based on getting more roofs to build and not doing the roofing work themselves.

(Alex hasn't hired an additional waitress yet, but he seems more conscious of the value of his own time and has started to pay more attention to his management duties. Old habits are hard to change, but that's a start.)

Changing employee attitudes

One of the most helpless feelings that a small business owner can have is not being able to find and keep the type of employees the business needs. It's a feeling that Bob and Dolores have quite often.

Most of Bob and Dolores' employees are sales clerks. They must know about the merchandise and be attentive to customers' needs. The financial structure of the retail store allows only a very modest pay scale for sales clerks. Bob and Dolores have learned from experience that they are unable to hire full-time sales clerks of the caliber they need. Their solution has been to use part time employees. They find most of their employees among students, retirees, or women whose children are in school.

"The problem is that when Bob and I are not around, not much work gets done and customer service suffers," said Dolores. "We have some friends that we have shop the store at times when we're not there. They tell us that customers are often ignored while our employees gossip with each other. We have a store manager, but it doesn't seem to help. Maybe we need a new one."

I was reminded of a case of a client who had a business in two cities—Chicago and New York. He would spend his time travelling, usually spending a week or two at a time in each city. He began to notice that profits in each city would increase during the period he was there. Conversely, profits in the other city would fall. Since he was not directly involved in either operation, it was quite a mystery to him.

I asked him who was in charge of his Chicago office when he was there. He said that he was. I asked him who was in charge of that office when he was in New York. He said that Tom, the office manager, was in charge. I disagreed. It was pretty apparent to me that my client, a forceful, take-charge type of guy, was the boss. When he was gone, there was no boss.

Whenever the owner is on the premises, he or she will be the boss unless it has been clearly established that the manager should continue to manage. So Bob and Dolores are the bosses and when they leave there is no boss. They might as well be in New York with my other client.

This is a situation that needs to be corrected or the business will suffer. The sales clerks are the only people that most customers deal with in Bob and Dolores' store. How the sales clerks act will determine how most customers view the store. Sullen or indifferent clerks will drive customers away, never to return.

The usual solution to this type of problem is to fire the employees or the manager or both. However, the cycle is likely to repeat itself over and over again. Continual hiring and training is expensive and disruptive. The level of performance will never be what you expect. The only way to break the cycle is to change employee attitudes.

Changing attitudes is not easy but the rewards are large. The first step is to make sure employees understand their jobs and the importance of this from the owner's point of view. The sales clerks create the customers' impression of the store, but most of Bob and Dolores' clerks did not act as if they understood this, or cared.

The role of the owner is to define the job and Bob and Dolores needed to do more work here. How were these inexperienced students supposed to make a favorable impression on the customers? Service is what Bob and Dolores really sell, yet most of these kids have spent their entire lives in self-service supermarkets. They don't know what real customer service is. Customer service has become a lost art. Dolores started to do training classes on how to wait on a customer. The results were immediate and dramatic. Service got better.

Most employees want responsibilities, and they want those responsibilities clearly defined. Most employees want to learn and grow. Bob took these facts into consideration and came up with a plan in which each employee, including the part time staff, became responsible for a specific section of merchandise. Responsibilities included merchandise displays, keeping merchandise fresh, taking inventory, and reordering. In addition, each employee was challenged to become an expert on his or her merchandise. As a section was mastered, an employee was assigned additional sections. Over time, the employee's stature in the store was determined by the number of sections that had been mastered.

People also want to share in success. Bob and Dolores worked out an incentive program that would pay employees for good performance. They also started running contests which emphasized customer service goals.

Every owner I've ever worked with was deeply concerned about his or her employees. An owner realizes the pay check is an important source of the income which defines the standard of living of the employee. The owner really wants the employee to succeed. But many times owners fail to communicate this. In fact, that is the biggest problem in employee relations. Bob has begun a program of periodic meetings with each employee to evaluate performance and get employee feedback and ideas.

Employee attitude really is improving. Employee

turnover is half of what it was last year. The reports from the secret visits of friends are so good that they are getting dull. I'm not known by the employees so recently I stopped in to look for a book and to check out the store. I gave the clerks a hard time and the bigger pain that I became, the nicer they treated me. I had the impression that they had a class operation to which I would want to return.

Partnerships

One way to make sure that employees share the owner's attitude is to make them owners. This is one reason why business partnerships are so popular. A partnership can often help a business grow much faster than a one-owner business. This is especially true when the partners are also working employees in the business. There is added potential because the owners are able to do so much. While the many advantages of partnerships are alluring, it is crucial to recognize the potential hazards. There needs to be a clear and ongoing understanding of the relationship. I consider partner relationship issues as important as sales or finances. If the partners are not getting along, there will be big trouble in the business.

When two people form a partnership, there is a strong implication that everything is 50-50. If one partner does bring more and the 50-50 arrangement doesn't apply, the partners should make a detailed agreement about their partnership before they get started.

When partners are also employees the 50-50 assumption comes under special strain. Is what one partner does equal to the other partner's contribution? Do they put in the same number of hours? How are they to be paid?

If the partners don't have a clear understanding of how this will work, the potential for conflict is great. The most absurd case I ever witnessed was one in which each partner started to do less and less because they both perceived that the other partner was dogging it. Luckily the partnership broke up before the business failed.

Mike and Jim are quite a successful partnership. They claim that their partnership is based on friendship and trust and all they have ever needed is a handshake. They have no written agreement between them. They've been operating this way for ten years so it makes my advice of having a clear understanding look rather foolish. It may be the exception that proves the rule.

Mike and Jim have been able to accomplish a lot together. They each have made a very nice living from the business. Jim's interest is in the administration of the business, and Mike's work is in the technical computer production phase. Their day to day employment duties are at least somewhat defined and separated.

Occasionally, I get to witness one of their partnership fights. Actually, they use our meetings as the time to formally talk to each other, as well as to consult with me. Without these meetings, it's possible that they wouldn't really talk to each other for months. A big communication problem could surface.

There are problems beginning to surface on a day to day basis. Jim is putting in many more hours on the job than Mike. This is a change. They both used to work long hours, but now Mike seems to be losing interest in the business. He's already told us about his plan to go back to school to get a

Ph.D. Jim is beginning to become resentful of Mike's leaving early every day. If Mike was just an employee, his absentee-ism would be confronted directly. But Mike is a partner. Does that change how the matter can be handled? Of course it does. That's why communication between partners is so important.

The Sales Savior

This potential partnership dispute is not likely to flare up as long as the business still has the "big problem." Jim and Mike must diversify their sales to get beyond Mr. Retailer. The one area of their business that they've never been able to establish is sales. They don't even have a sales person in their employ.

They do have independent sales representatives in some areas of the country. These are independent contractors who call on local retailers on behalf of a number of manufac-turers and receive a commission on their sales.

Both Mike and Jim have a vague vision of what sounds like a sales "savior." This is a person who would take charge of sales so they wouldn't need to be involved. The sales savior would be expected to solve the sales problem once and for all. In return Mike and Jim would make the ultimate sacrifice by paying this superstar "big bucks."

Every so often they put an ad in the Wall Street Journal classified, but most of the time they don't even open the inquiries they get from potential candidates. I'm not sure why. But I am sure they don't want to commit to paying a high salary and it's possible they are afraid of success. If the salesman really succeeded, they may have another partner whether they want one or not. A person with control over sales could threaten to leave and take customers along.

As we've seen in this chapter, business success is often based on adding key employees. But as Mike and Jim are finding out, the direction of the business must be defined before a new job can be identified. Let's examine how our friends go about making decisions about their future.

*"You'll never accomplish much
more than you plan to."*

206

CHAPTER TWELVE

Decisions About the Future:
What Do I Want to Do When I Grow Up
(Or Even Next Year)?

You won't accomplish much more than you plan to

A new client came to me complaining about her disappointing profits in the previous year. As I questioned her, I learned that she had a good little business that seemed to be very well run. The problem was that, though she had been in business for eight years, her profits were barely enough to stay alive. "What level of profit did you plan to make?" I asked innocently. She hesitated for a moment and then told me that she really didn't have a plan.

Sometimes my sense of humor gets the best of me and before I could stop myself I said, "Gosh, since you didn't plan to make any money, you really did better than you thought you would."

My wisecrack wasn't intended to embarrass the client, but it did. My simple response hit home and it shocked her a bit too. She had worked hard for many years without achieving the success she deserved.

Two years have passed since our first meeting. This client has now defined what she wants to accomplish and her profits have more than doubled each year. What's changed? She now makes plans for her business.

The basic rule of thumb is: You'll never accomplish much more than you plan to accomplish. So if you don't plan, you can accurately predict that in the future things will be about the same as they are now.

The small business owner's edge

Most people don't do much planning. It probably wouldn't do them a lot of good anyway, because most people are employed. If their plans don't coincide with their boss' plans, there's little opportunity to carry them out. For the small business owner, the opposite is true.

A small business owner is in a unique position. An owner can actually set goals and achieve them. Large companies try to do this, but often get pulled in many different directions. Of course, you never have absolute power to define your future. But as a small business owner you can come closer than anyone else. The opportunity to plan is a big advantage that small business owners have. If you don't use it, you are giving up this edge and hurting your chances for success.

Goal setting – pain and power

No one has ever claimed that planning was easy, and the hardest part is setting goals. The last easy goal you had was probably getting a diploma. Education is a great goal because everybody agrees it's something good. There is a prescribed plan to get it, and even a graduation date to aim at.

But what happens after graduation? Some people go after a fancy new car, or perhaps that house in the "burbs" with 2-1/2 children. For most people, the next important goal is retirement. If you think I'm being critical of the general motivation level of our society, you're right. Most people don't spend much time setting goals. It's too hard. So why should a small business owner be any different? Goal setting is certainly no easier for a small business owner, but it's more worthwhile because the goals can actually be achieved.

Most formal training for goal setting works toward five year goals. That's because most people are employed, and five years is a "safe" time frame which usually doesn't disturb current employment. Five year goals are fine if you can do them, but for most people it's much farther out than they want to or even can project in any detail. Almost every small business client I've had with strong five year goals has achieved them in three years or less. The key here is in how far we can project our goals and still be motivated to work hard on them. I've seen some people working seriously on 20 year goals. God bless them.

I took the position some years ago that each of my clients needed to have goals that were at least a year away. I'd like to see longer term goals but that is a workable minimum. Most owners respond well to setting goals one year out. They recognize that a year isn't that long a time, yet it is time enough to change anything they would like to change.

I like to have my clients actively working on their goals every six months. If every six months they are looking at goals about a year away, they have the opportunity to review what they've done and they don't end up having run out of goals.

Many small business owners need to be motivated to work regularly on goals. There is a natural resistance to working on long-term planning. But when you see a very successful business, you can bet that the owner has a strong habit of doing long-term planning. Business success is not accidental.

Planning without facts is guesswork

At the start-up stage of a business, there rarely is a lack of planning. The planning may not be effective, however, because there are too few facts. Facts are developed by taking action and until you actually start operating a business, planning is mostly guess work.

The closest analogy is probably a school teacher's first year of teaching. In most jobs, employees are trained and break in gradually. As they gain experience, they are promoted. But a school teacher is expected to perform at the highest level from day one, the same way a business is expected to perform even if it has just "opened its doors."

For better or for worse the start-up owner adopts a plan and then proceeds to implement it. The start-up plan is an act of faith. The owner charges ahead to carry it out regardless of the facts. What follows could be described as a period of insanity that usually lasts between six months and a year.

During the insanity period, the owner usually won't listen to anyone. The owner's sole intent is to carry out the plan. It does not matter if the business is succeeding or failing, the owner will execute the plan.

If the original guesswork plan was too unrealistic, the business may not last to the second year. Once the business does survive this initial period, the owner becomes more sensitive to what is actually happening in the business and is in a position to improve the planning. Unfortunately, by this time many owners are disillusioned because their original guesswork planning didn't turn out the way they expected. They may drop the planning tool at the very time they are learning enough facts to make it valuable.

"Am I over my year of insanity?" asked Susan. "I sometimes think I was nuts to go into business in the first place."

I teased her by saying that I thought that she was probably "off her rocker" long before she thought of going into business for herself. Actually Susan hadn't followed the usual start-up pattern. She had a plan, but she seemed to recognize when it was time to modify what she was doing to fit the circumstances. She was also a good listener. Perhaps the extensive business experience she'd had in the corporation made her different. She made about every mistake in the book, particularly in her marketing, but her decision-making skills were good.

By almost every measure, Susan has had a wonderful year. In her first year of business she has produced roughly double the income she had earned in her last year of employment. She's very happy and proud of herself and she should be. It was a remarkable first year performance.

The tough question is: "What about next year?" Susan's first year success was built by having one large account and several small ones. When the project she is doing for the large account ends, her revenues will virtually stop.

"How can I plan for next year?" asked Susan. "I won't know how next year will be until I get another 'big' account. There is no sense planning on something that I can't count on."

I agree with Susan's conclusion that she will have a difficult time planning the next year. But I disagree with her reasoning. Very few businesses really know what their specific sources of revenue will be in the next year unless there are already agreements in place. But most businesses have marketing programs which allow them to predict with some assurance what next year will be like.

What Susan is missing is a proven marketing program. She was able to get some nice business simply by talking with some of her old friends, but she has been so busy doing the work, she hasn't been able to even do that networking lately.

When she looks ahead, she sees a lot of unknowns. When this big job ends, it will bring up many questions. Was getting the big account in the first place was just a fluke? Will there ever be another account like this one? These are chilling questions that anyone who has ever owned a business has had to face from time to time. Until a business has developed a proven way to get new business, next year will always be uncertain. Maybe even next week.

I consider developing a consistent, marketing program to be the highest priority of a new business. The question is always, "Can we repeat this next year?"Susan has the basis for developing a reliable marketing program. She has many contacts, but those she doesn't use, she will lose.

This is a clear example of how necessary facts are to planning. If Susan knew how she could get more business, she could start making some firm plans about a new location, employees, and what her personal income would be. Since she doesn't know that yet, she is still like the start-up owner, and the planning is mostly guess work.

As long as her planning is still in this mode, you'd have to say that Susan is still planning for survival and not success. In fact, when you ask Susan what success is, she will say that she hopes to repeat this year, next year. She is stuck on survival. For most new businesses survival is the goal.

Susan's answer to the question, "What does it look like a year from now?", is having a proven marketing program in place. Once she attains that goal, she can probably accomplish whatever she wants to do.

Controlling the "Tidbits"

Every so often I run into people who tell me that they have long-term goals, but they don't write them down. They keep them in their heads. What they are telling me is that their future isn't important enough to them to write their goals down. Invariably, these owners have sub-par businesses and wonder why.

Here's a hot tip for you if you'd like to cut some money from your food budget. Make out a grocery list. Lists work! Lists are the great aid to planning.

Depending on the nature of your business, you may need to do a daily task list. This focuses your efforts and you'll find that you accomplish more.

Years ago, I stumbled upon a planning technique that fills a gap between the daily task list and the long-term goals. For lack of a better name, I called it "priority planning." Then one day a client was describing his feelings about not being organized and feeling out of control. He said that he sensed there were "tidbits" of information floating all around that he needed but couldn't quite grasp.

I recognized immediately that he was describing exactly the purpose of the "priority planning" which was to get control of all those "tidbits." Henceforth, it became the "tidbit list."

The most important part of a tidbit list is that you need to set aside a specific time each week to do it. That time truly becomes priority time. Nothing must be allowed to interfere with it. I work on my tidbit list very early on Sunday morning—the only time there is nobody hassling me. I've been doing this for ten years and I consider it a key secret to my success. On those rare occasions when someone is unlucky enough to interrupt me, I'm likely to act like a small child throwing a tantrum.

The reason that I don't want my concentration broken is that the quality of my Sunday morning planning often determines the quality of my week. If I do a dynamite job of planning, it will be a great week and the reverse is often true. It's magic!

The main reason it's important to pick a time for planning is to make sure that you do it. However, there are other benefits. I know that I'll be planning next Sunday morning, so if I come up with an idea or with an important decision that doesn't have to be acted upon immediately, I'll defer it to Sunday morning. At that time I'll have all my ideas and needs together and I can make balanced judgments and therefore, good decisions.

I spend my week in action, not planning. The planning is done on Sunday mornings. And, I never lose an idea. An idea goes on the tidbit list. Every idea gets evaluated and if it's worthwhile it gets acted upon.

My tidbit list techniques include starting with a blank piece of paper. (I find this more productive than pulling up last week's list on a computer screen.) I start by identifying those major tasks that I need to tackle during the next week. I don't list my basic job which is seeing clients. A typical tidbit might be, "write Chapter 12," or "prepare marketing talk." Then I list those projects or ideas that I probably won't get to work on for a while. This could be developing a mailing list to be used in three months or deciding what discussion groups to offer during the coming year. It also includes those long-term ideas that I won't do anything about in the foreseeable future, but I don't want to lose track of. Sometimes a longer term idea will fit an emerging need and it will be put into action immediately. The idea for this book was very low on my tidbit lists for almost a year. But if it hadn't been on those lists, the book would probably not exist today.

After I write down my current ideas, I look over the list from last week to see if there is anything I've forgotten. I try to figure out what the priorities are and make my decisions.

Sometimes there will be something on your tidbit list that you should be doing but you are not. The first question should be, "Do I still want to do it?" If you do, the next question is, "Have I identified the next step that needs to be taken?" Often that is what's stopping you. For example, if I list "Do January newsletter," absolutely nothing will happen, because that's too big a task. To get the newsletter going, I have to break it down into "update mailing list," and "do first draft."

I encourage you to try the tidbit list approach as I've outlined it. It will pay you over and over again for the time you spend on it. It might even change your life. It sure has changed mine.

What is success?

Cindy is the type of person who has always made grocery lists and now she's running her business with lists, too. Her systems are beginning to pay off. It took her only six months to reach the goals that she had planned to reach in 12 months.

I asked her if she was going to take the rest of the year off, since she has already attained her goals.

"It does look like I underestimated what we would do this year," replied Cindy, "How should I go about setting goals? Is there a better way? Until now, my approach has been to base my goals on the business I did this year with something added for growth."

Last year's performance should be a factor in determining goals, but only a factor. I think that if your goal is simply to increase business 25%, you are missing the real advantage of setting goals. Setting goals is your opportunity to define your future. You are only limited by your imagination. Your goals should be exciting to you. So, what excites you?

A small business owner has business <u>and</u> personal goals. Both should be considered. The business may be looked upon as a way to achieve your personal goals. Or the business may provide some exciting challenges of its own.

Don't hesitate to use a personal goal to inspire your business goals. Most owners work too many hours. Set a goal to get more leisure time. Improve the business enough so that you can afford someone to replace you during your "off" time. Then actually take the time off when you meet your goal.

Goals should be realistic. You must be able to believe you can achieve them. Moreover, you should be able to lay out specific plans. Goals are not just pie in the sky dreams.

One of the most important rules about setting goals is to identify the date of accomplishment. A goal without a date really isn't a goal. Ask yourself, "What does it look like next year on this date?" I asked Cindy the same question in another way: "What is success?"

Cindy's goals are somewhat confused. She has already achieved much more with her moving business than she ever thought she would, but she has gone nowhere with her singing career. She treats it as if the moving business is something that she will do until she grows up and then she will turn into a singer.

Clearly her full concentration and commitment has been on building the moving business and she has succeeded in making it a viable business. Up to now her success has been closely tied to survival. That usually is the way it is in the early years of a new business.

What will excite Cindy? Will she want to expand the moving business by adding more trucks and employees? Will she back track and put more time into her singing career?

Is there yet another direction that Cindy would like to go? These are decisions that Cindy will have to make and that will determine her direction. Just having those kinds of choices is exciting.

The 21 square plan—time control

Alex's idea of long term planning is working up his menus for the next week. Once I coaxed him to define some goals, and he tried, but it was obvious that he didn't take them seriously or believe in them. Habits built up over the years are hard to change overnight. Alex has struggled for so long that he really believes he always will. As long as he thinks this way, Alex will always struggle.

Changes in the last year have somewhat disrupted Alex's negative patterns. The extra profits from after-the-movie business have allowed him to pay his bills. He has more time because half of his time used to be spent avoiding and fighting with bill collectors. This, together with his decision not to be a full-time waiter in his own restaurant, has freed up much of his time. So far he is mostly wasting that time.

There are many things Alex can do to improve business, ranging from promotional schemes to doing more cooking himself. The problem is he has lost control of his time. He has an appointment book but he never looks at it. My internal procedures, for instance, have always been to call Alex in the morning to remind him of our meeting that day. Otherwise he would never show up at the meeting because of his disorganization.

There's a technique I learned some years ago that's

helpful to an owner who doesn't have extensive pre-defined time. I can't use it myself because I see a number of clients each day and I live by my appointment book. Called "21 squares," this technique has proven very useful to most consultants who work on big projects for large clients and for owners of retail stores who have plenty of tasks but no predefined times when they must do them. This fits Alex' new situation.

To develop your 21 squares, simply write each day of the week across the top of a piece of paper. Then divide the sheet roughly into three equal sections horizontally and write "morning," "afternoon" and "evening" down the left side. Draw lines between the days and the sections and you will have created 21 squares: morning, afternoon, and evening for seven days. Think of this as 21 opportunities to work. Some people will prefer not to work on Sunday, so that means 18 opportunities to work.

The 21 square system works best for someone who looks ahead at a typical week and sees only a couple of commitments—perhaps a lunch on Wednesday and a meeting with a customer on Thursday afternoon. This 21 square calendar becomes a planning tool to define how to spend the rest of the week in the most productive fashion.

To my great surprise, Alex not only tried the 21 square system, he adopted it like a long-lost rich relative. He began to use 21 squares to define all his time. He uses it to schedule his employees' work hours, plan menus, and buy food. He has set up an office full of 21 squares. The system has replaced "billions" of small pieces of paper.

If a man can go to the moon, could Alex someday start planning his business? One small step...

The value of the big goal

Strong goals create an irresistible force, because goals mean both motivation and direction. Motivation gives people a reason to do something, and direction helps them determine what to do. For Bob and Dolores the idea of retirement in five years became a strong goal. It was obvious that the business had to improve to achieve that goal, and this had the effect of putting a "burr under their saddles." Even though they had formerly had a good business, they had not been applying themselves to making it a better business. Apparently there was no reason for them to do so. Now there is.

I'm convinced that the biggest reason a business is a given size is that it is the size that fits the owner's imagination. In other words, your business will probably only grow to the size you can visualize.

If you have trouble visualizing the future, try to find role models. If you can find successful situations that you'd like to emulate, it can be like having an instant burst of imaginative thinking. Without an identified target the future can be pretty murky. The role model helps you identify how you'd like your future to be. Once you identify that target, goal setting gets a lot easier.

Bob and Dolores were able to reduce their retirement vision to a "money" goal, and then they devised a plan to make the money they needed. They made it work. It's a simple formula. Just add new motivation and new direction to years of experience and then jump out of the way so you won't be run over.

The five year plan that Bob and Dolores had put together was accomplished in 3-1/2 years. They did sell the store and today they are retired.

In one of our last meetings, Bob was exhausted but very proud of what they'd accomplished. "Next time around I think I'd have a lot more special sales," he reflected. I asked if there would be a next time—what had he planned to do? He said he hadn't finalized plans because he was so busy selling the store. I thought that was sad because it was obvious that this couple can do whatever they plan to do, but they don't have a plan, so...

Why businesses stop growing

Goals are fairly obvious at certain stages of a business. When starting up, the immediate goal is survival. You hope that the survival goal is achieved quickly or else the business won't be nearly as much fun as it could be.

Often, the next stage of growth is fueled by the need of the owner to achieve the standard of living to which he or she has become accustomed. In these first two stages the motivating emotion is often fear—usually fear of failure.

Once the necessary standard of living has been achieved, the owner must look elsewhere for motivation. Actually fear can still be a motivator. Mike and Jim are primary examples because their business can be crippled by the decisions of their biggest customer. Hence, fear drives the goal to diversify.

While diversifying the business is something that Mike and Jim still need to do, it's been a goal for so long that perhaps it has lost some of its meaning. After all, the situation has not changed for years. They keep making more money.

The urgency to diversify has weakened though the need is still there.

Sometimes making a change in direction in an established business is much harder than starting something new from scratch. Sometimes habits have to be unlearned before a new direction can proceed.

The idea of selling games by mail is an exciting new goal for Mike and Jim. If they can establish a successful mail order business, they will no longer be under the thumb of Mr. Retailer. They'll be able to sleep better at night.

Despite the incentive to get it going, the mail order business hasn't gotten off the ground. There is no question that Mike and Jim want to do it, but they haven't spent the time they should have to plan the new venture. It's much easier for them to just keep doing their day-to-day work.

This may be the single biggest reason why businesses stop growing. The owners don't do the planning they need to do. I've seen it happening to dozens of businesses. Exciting goals and a hard push are often needed to get a business moving.

(Mike and Jim have broken through this planning barrier before and they will again. They will find out if the mail order business can be successful.)

Only your imagination limits you

An owner must have fresh, exciting goals or the business will never reach its potential. They must be the owner's goals, because you can't give anyone else your goals. At the same time, I try to give my clients ideas that may stimulate them to come up with goals of their own. Some years ago I put a list of ideas in my newsletter. It read:

- "When it's 20 below in Chicago in January, how would you like to be basking in the Caribbean sun?
- "Suppose your business was so established that your banker would call you about next year's working capital needs?
- "What if you could afford to hire that key person who would really take the pressure off you?
  "Paris in the spring! Ever tried it?
- "Suppose you built your business so that you could sell it for big bucks and go teach or pick daisies or something?
- "What if you could give a large endowment to a school, or a social movement, or medical research?
- "How about another TV, VCR, PC, CD or even a BMW?
- "Perhaps you should increase your personal income to $100,000? Or $200,000?
- "What if you were famous or at least respected enough so that Ted Koppel would interview you on "Nightline?"
- "Suppose you woke up one morning and didn't have a single past due bill?
- "Or, maybe you just want more time with your kids or your sweetheart or breathing the beautiful fresh air.

The above list is about your goals and dreams. Let's all go into 1990 knowing what we want to accomplish."

The first year I published this list I got many favorable comments. A year later while reviewing materials to put in my fall newsletter, I reread the list and realized that in the last year everyone of those goals had been achieved by at least one of my clients. I think the list helps some clients identify their goals and so every year I republish this list with appropriate additions and deletions. It still works.

What excites you?

As we've examined the crucial decisions in a business, we've seen a lot of "secrets" of success. If you were to ask me to name the most important one, I'd say without hesitation— "the excitement of the owner."

An excited owner will overcome many failings in a business. Failures are a part of doing business. When you take action you either succeed or fail. Regardless of which happens, you have the opportunity to learn from the results. A profitable business is built through the learning experiences. An excited owner is able to overcome failures or live with successes and continue to learn.

So what excites you? Goals do. You need reasons to do what you are doing. The stronger the reasons, the better goals they will be for you.

Dare to dream. It won't be easy. Often those closest to you will try to protect you. They'll give you all kinds of good reasons not to go ahead with your dream. What are they protecting you from? Failure.

If you dare to dream and to take action on your dreams, you will sometimes fail. So what? All that means is that you will need to try again. Guess what? You'll probably fail again. But, you'll learn.

When I was at the idea stage with virtually everything I do today, those closest to me thought they were bad ideas. And I certainly had a lot of doubts and early failures as I tested the business.

At the same time, I was excited. I could see that I was helping people. I could see that my success was based on other people's success. This created such a thrilling atmosphere that the failures never mattered much. In fact, the failures showed me how to establish better procedures for the business.

Yes, you can make a 1,000 poor decisions and still succeed. All you have to do is to recognize the <u>crucial</u> decisions and give them the full attention they deserve. If that occasionally means getting help, then do it. With the crucial decisions under control, you'll be ready to follow your dreams.

Above all, dare to dream. Find out what excites you.

AUTHOR'S NOTES

Will Susan continue her successful start-up?

Will Cindy sell her business and become a professional singer?

Will Alex continue to survive?

How will Bob and Dolores adjust to retirement, and what about the folks who bought the store from them?

Will Mike and Jim remain partners, and will they ever diversify the business?

I've become so attached to our friends that I'm going to continue to write about their further adventures. So if you'd like to follow their stories, write for your free newsletter.

Write: Newsletter
                                The Wright Track
                                P. O. Box 3416
                                Oak Park, IL 60303

Harold L. Wright
Founder and President
THE WRIGHT TRACK FOR
SMALL BUSINESS SUCCESS

Ironically, The Wright Track didn't begin as part of a master plan. It started accidentally when a small business owner asked Harold (Hal) Wright for help with her business.

In working with that owner, Hal discovered that an objective, informed advisor who focused on the combined planning of marketing, finances, and personnel could help make a good business better

It worked so well that as The Wright Track grew Hal was able to base his fees on the results he helped create. This meant that he could work with the smallest of businesses—those that ordinarily could not afford to work with a professional advisor. Thus Hal had the opportunity to advise hundreds of small business owners in the Chicago area. The word spread and Hal now has clients in almost every part of the country.

Hal's varied experience includes small business ownership, corporate level management, and background as an attorney, accountant, and financial planner. He is a graduate of the University of Iowa and of Chicago-Kent College of Law

Hal is writing a second book in which he will share his techniques for advising small business owners. His new book should be helpful to accountants, lawyers, bankers and others who advise entrepreneurs

Dear Robert,

I hope this book
will help you to
even greater success.

Hal Wright
4-3-90